A Practical Facilities Maintenance Handbook

KEVIN JONES

A Practical Facilities Maintenance Handbook

© 2024 Kevin Jones Some Rights Reserved & the moral rights of the author to be identified as the originator of the work are also asserted.

A Practical Facilities Maintenance Handbook by Kevin Jones is licensed under Creative Commons Attribution-Share Alike International License CC BY-SA 4.0.

To view a copy of this license, visit: https://creativecommons.org/licenses/by-sa/4.0/

I, Kevin Jones the author/illustrator of this handbook, hereby grant permission to reproduce, store in a retrieval system, transmit, in any form or by any means, electronic or photocopy, or otherwise, any part of this handbook. If any of the 3D graphics, or isometric shop equipment drawings are reproduced or transmitted in any form or by any means, electronic or photocopy, or otherwise, credit is to be sighted as follows: *A Practical Facilities Maintenance Handbook, By Kevin Jones.*

Disclaimer: By purchasing, reading, or using any of the material in this handbook, you agree to hold harmless the author, Kevin Jones from any legal or financial liability or responsibility for property damage, or bodily injury that may occur as a result of using this handbook.

First published in the United States of America in 2024

Printed & bound in the United States of America in 2024

ISBN: 979-8-218-98434-2 (eBook)

ISBN: 979-8-218-98360-4 (Paperback)

LCCN: 2024916281

Table of Contents

1. Introduction
2. Request for Proposal
3. Request for Quote
4. Work Order
5. Daily Forklift Inspection Log
6. Facility Inspection
7. Bill of Materials/Cut List
8. Training Roster
9. Vehicle Inspection
10. Monthly Fire Service & Quarterly Test Log
11. Water Quality Monitoring Log
12. Temperature Log
13. Hot Work Permit
14. Confined Space Entrance Permit
15. Refrigerant Usage Log
16. Exit & Entrance Signs
17. No Parking Sign
18. No Smoking Sign
19. Closed for Maintenance Sign
20. Wet Paint
21. Empty & Arrow Signs
22. Lockout/Tagout Tags
23. Inspection Record Tags
24. Maintenance Record Tags
25. HAZMAT & HAZWASTE Labels
26. HAZCOM Secondary Container Labels
27. NFPA Diamond & GHS Pictograms Key
28. Welding Symbols
29. Plumbing Symbols
30. Electrical Symbols
31. Wire Gauge & Ampacity
32. 3-Way Switch Wiring Diagram
33. Receptacle & Plug Wiring Diagram
34. Thermostat Wiring Diagram
35. HVAC Refrigerant Circuit
36. Furnace Sequence of Operation
37. Troubleshooting Flowchart
38. How to Reduce Waste in Your Facility
39. Weights, Measures, Formulas
40. Chain & Sling Storage Rack
41. Parts Rack
42. Work Bench
43. Kidney-Loop Filtration & Transfer Cart
44. Self-Dumping Hopper
45. Spool Storage Rack
46. 55-Gal. Drum Lube Cart
47. Oil Filter Crusher & Absorbent Pad Wringer
48. Aerosol Can Recycle System
49. Mop Water Reclamation System
50. Oil Skimmers
51. Mobile Drain Pan & Rotating Build Stand
52. Stationary Oil Reclaim System
53. Inches to Millimeters Conversion Table
54. Glossary of Terms & Abbreviations
55. Glossary of Terms & Abbreviations Cont.
56. About the Author

Introduction

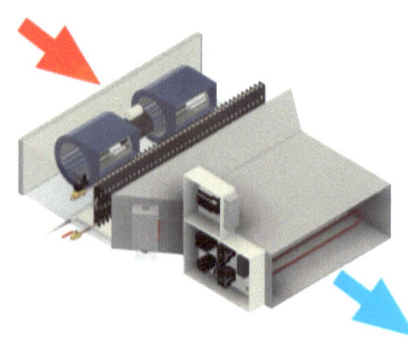

A Practical Facilities Maintenance Handbook has been designed as your go-to source for documents, signage, tags, labels, and reference materials that are commonly used in the facilities maintenance/management space. Since no two facilities are exactly the same, it would be impractical to try and fill this handbook with every possible piece of content that every facility may use. Instead, the content in this handbook is designed to be universal in nature. The purpose of this handbook is to improve workflows, increase productivity and safety of employees and building occupants.

The content of this handbook was carefully curated. Examples of commonly used documents included in this handbook are: work order, request for quote, request for proposal, hot work permit, daily forklift inspection, and more. These documents can be photocopied and used as is, or you can scan them into your computer and add your company logo and company details to each form to make them your own. Examples of commonly used signage, tags, and labels included in this handbook are: no parking, closed for maintenance, wet paint, hazmat, lockout/tagout, inspection tags, secondary container tags, and more. These all can be used as is, or printed and laminated, or even printed on sticker paper. Additionally, included in this handbook is an inches-to-millimeters conversion table, wiring schematics, welding, plumbing, and electrical symbols, and 3D isometric drawings of common shop equipment that you can use to fabricate your own shop equipment in house, or send the drawings to your local metal shop to fabricate for your facility.

Request For Proposal

FROM:

TO:

REQUEST DATE:

REQUEST #:

ADDRESS CORRESPONDENCE TO:

TERMS/CONDITIONS:

Proposal Name:

Proposal Description/Goals:

Scope of Work:

Timeline:

_____ _____
SIGNATURE   **DATE**

Request For Quote

FROM:

TO:

REQUEST DATE:

REQUEST #:

ADDRESS CORRESPONDENCE TO:

TERMS/CONDITIONS:

Qty	Description	Part #	Cost
			Total:

SIGNATURE   **DATE**

Work Order

Work Order #:	Date of Assignment:
Equipment ID:	Expected Completion Date:
Location:	Priority Level:
Assigned to:	Maintenance Type:

Description of Work Required:
Tools/Equipment/Parts/Materials Required:
Safety Guidelines:
Work Completion Notes:
Total Hours to Complete:

Signed Print Date

Daily Forklift Inspection Record

Forklift: _____ Month: _____ Year: _____

☑ PASS ☒ FAIL

	1	2	3	4	5	6	7	8	9	10	11	12	13	14	15	16	17	18	19	20	21	22	23	24	25	26	27	28	29	30	31
Inspect Overhead Guard																															
Inspect Mast/Forks/Carriage																															
Inspect Hyd. Cylinders/Hoses																															
Inspect Wheels/Tires																															
Check Fluid Levels																															
Check Battery/Cables																															
Check Belts/Hoses																															
Check Fuel Level or Battery Charge																															
Does the Seatbelt Work?																															
Owners Manual onboard?																															
Does the Horn Work?																															
Does Forklift Start?																															
Do the Lights & Gauges Work?																															
Does the Backup Alarm Work?																															
Steering & Directional Control Work?																															
Do the Service Brakes & Parking Brake Work?																															
Does the Hydraulic Controls Work?																															

Immediately report any unsafe condition to management. Do not operate an unsafe forklift. Lockout/Tagout an unsafe forklift.

(OSHA 1910.178 Compliance)

Facility Inspection

Inspector Name:	
Inspection Date:	
Facility Location/ID:	

ITEM	NOTES
Walls	
Flooring	
Ceilings	
Roof	
Doors/Windows	
Electrical	
Plumbing	
HVAC	
Lighting	
Emergency Equipment	
Security Equipment	
Restrooms	
Kitchens	
Laundry Room	
Equipment Room	
Electrical Room	
Janitor's Closet	
Maintenance Shop	
Parking Lot/Garage	
Furniture	
Landscaping	
Pool/Spa	
Gym	
Cafeteria/Lunchroom	

Signature

Date

Bill of Materials/Cut List

Project Name:	Total Cost:
Prepared By:	Approved By:
Date:	Approval Date:

Project Description: _____

_____

_____

Item #	Qty. Req.	Item Name	Description/Part#	Cost	Extended	Supplier
					Total:	

Notes: _____

_____

_____

Training Roster

Training Topic: _____

Training Date: _____

Trainer: _____

Name	Name

Vehicle Inspection

Inspector Name:	
Inspection Date:	
Vehicle ID:	Mileage:

ITEM	NOTES
Exterior	
Interior	
Rims/Tires/Lug Nuts	
Wiper Blades	
Lights	
Mirrors	
Service Brakes	
Parking Brake	
Fluids	
Battery/Cables	
Belts/Hoses	
HVAC	
Transmission Operation	
Engine Operation	
Current Registration	
Current Insurance	
Service History	
Emergency Equipment	

_____ _____
Signature   **Date**

Monthly Elevator Fire Service & Quarterly Two-Way Communication Test Log

Building ID:

Elevator ID:

Year:

Date	Phase 1		Phase 2		Two-Way Com.		Initials
	☐Pass	☐Fail	☐Pass	☐Fail	☐Pass	☐Fail	
	☐Pass	☐Fail	☐Pass	☐Fail	☐Pass	☐Fail	
	☐Pass	☐Fail	☐Pass	☐Fail	☐Pass	☐Fail	
	☐Pass	☐Fail	☐Pass	☐Fail	☐Pass	☐Fail	
	☐Pass	☐Fail	☐Pass	☐Fail	☐Pass	☐Fail	
	☐Pass	☐Fail	☐Pass	☐Fail	☐Pass	☐Fail	
	☐Pass	☐Fail	☐Pass	☐Fail	☐Pass	☐Fail	
	☐Pass	☐Fail	☐Pass	☐Fail	☐Pass	☐Fail	
	☐Pass	☐Fail	☐Pass	☐Fail	☐Pass	☐Fail	
	☐Pass	☐Fail	☐Pass	☐Fail	☐Pass	☐Fail	
	☐Pass	☐Fail	☐Pass	☐Fail	☐Pass	☐Fail	
	☐Pass	☐Fail	☐Pass	☐Fail	☐Pass	☐Fail	

Immediately notify your maintenance contractor if there is a failure of the fire service, or quarterly two-way communication test!

Contractor Phone #: _____

Water Quality Monitoring Log

Equipment ID:	Location:
Month:	Year:

Date	Time	Employee	Water In Temp	Water Out Temp	Ph (ppm)	Alk (ppm)	TDS (ppm)	Conduct. (µS)	Salinity (ppm)

Notes:_____

Temperature Log

Date	Name	Location	Equipment ID	Temp. Before Adjustment	Temp. After Adjustment

NOTES:_____

HOT WORK PERMIT

Required by NFPA 51B & ANSI Z49.1

Seek an alternative method if possible!

A hot work permit is required for any work procedure involving open flame, heat, or sparks. This includes, but is not limited to: welding, cutting, brazing, soldering, grinding, chemical welding, torch applied heating.

DATE:	THIS PERMIT IS VALID FOR	☐ ONE DAY	☐ ONE WEEK	☐ ONE MONTH

Hot work to be done by: ☐ Employee ☐ Contractor
Name of person doing hot work:
Location of hot work:
Description of hot work:
I, the (PAI) permit-authorizing individual, hereby verify that the location mentioned herein this permit has been examined and the required safety precautions herein have been implemented. My signature below grants permission to the person doing hot work.
(PAI) permit-authorizing individual:

Safety Precautions:

- ☐ Available & operable fire extinguisher(s), hose streams, fire sprinklers.
- ☐ Hot work equipment is in good working condition per the manufacturer's specifications.
- ☐ Special permission to conduct hot work on metal vessels and/or piping lined with rubber or plastic.
- ☐ Flammable liquid, dust, and oily deposits have been removed within 35 feet of hot work.
- ☐ Hot work area floor swept clean and free of trash/trip hazards.
- ☐ All applicable wall and floor openings are covered.
- ☐ Welding screens and fume extraction devices are in place to protect effected personnel.
- ☐ Combustible floors wet down or covered with damp sand or fire resistive/non-combustible materials.
- ☐ Personnel are protected from electrical shock when floors are wet.
- ☐ Other combustible materials have been removed or covered with listed fire resistive materials.
- ☐ Ducts or conveyors that might carry sparks to distant combustible materials have been covered/shutdown.
- ☐ Hot work on walls/ceilings/roofs: Material is non-combustible or moved away from the wall/ceiling/roof.
- ☐ Hot work on enclosed equipment: Equipment is clean of all combustibles.
- ☐ Hot work on enclosed equipment: Containers are purged of flammable liquid/vapor.
- ☐ Hot work on enclosed equipment: pressured vessels/piping/equipment have been isolated or vented.
- ☐ A fire watch will be provided during hot work & 1 hour after hot work is completed. Including break periods.
- ☐ A fire watch is equipped with suitable extinguishers, and hose if needed.
- ☐ The fire watch is trained how to use the equipment and sound an alarm if needed.
- ☐ Additional fire watch personnel required in adjoining areas?   ☐ YES   ☐ NO
- ☐ Per the PAI/fire watch, monitoring of hot work has been extended beyond 1 hour?   ☐ YES   ☐ NO

CONFINED SPACE ENTRY PERMIT

Required by OSHA 29 CFR 1910.146

Seek an alternative method if possible!

A confined space entry permit is required for any work performed in a confined space that meets the criteria of OSHA 29 CFR 1919.146.

DATE:		THIS PERMIT IS VALID FOR	☐ ONE DAY	☐ ONE WEEK	☐ ONE MONTH

Confined space work to be done by: ☐ Employee ☐ Contractor
Authorized confined space entrant:
Authorized safety standby attendant:
Location of confined space:
Description of work in confined space:
I, the (PAI) permit-authorizing individual, hereby verify that the location mentioned herein this permit has been examined and the required safety precautions herein have been implemented. My signature below grants permission to work in the confined space.
(PAI) permit-authorizing individual:

Communication Procedures	☐ RADIO/CELL	☐ VOICE	☐ LIFELINE	☐ VISUAL

Entrant contact info.	
Attendant contact info.	

Rescue Procedure:

PRE-ENTRY SAFETY CHECKLIST

- ☐ Equipment has been deenergized and locked out/tagged out
- ☐ Lines broken and/or capped
- ☐ Purge-flush and vent
- ☐ Secured area (post & flag)
- ☐ Ventilation: test & monitor for oxygen levels, flammability, toxicity, explosive hazards before/during entry
- ☐ Breathing Apparatus
- ☐ Resuscitator and Inhalator
- ☐ Standby safety personnel
- ☐ Full body harness
- ☐ Emergency escape retrieval equipment
- ☐ PPE
- ☐ Lifelines
- ☐ Explosion-proof lighting
- ☐ Fire extinguisher(s)
- ☐ Hot Work Permit if applicable

Refrigerant Usage Log

A hardcopy of this log worksheet is to be kept on file with the refrigerant program for three years

DATE	REFRIGERANT	QUANTITY RECOVERED OR CHARGED	EQ. #	EQUIPMENT NAME	W/O#	LOCATION	REMARKS	INITIALS

Total ounces reclaimed/recycled _____ (only list refrigerant that was removed from the site and **not** reused in existing equipment)

Total ounces of refrigerant consumed _____ (new refrigerant added due to leaks and repairs)

EXIT

ENTRANCE

NO
PARKING

NO

SMOKING

CLOSED

FOR

MAINTENANCE

WET

PAINT

EMPTY

Inspection Record

Item: _____

DATE	NAME

Inspection Record

Item: _____

DATE	NAME

Inspection Record

Item: _____

DATE	NAME

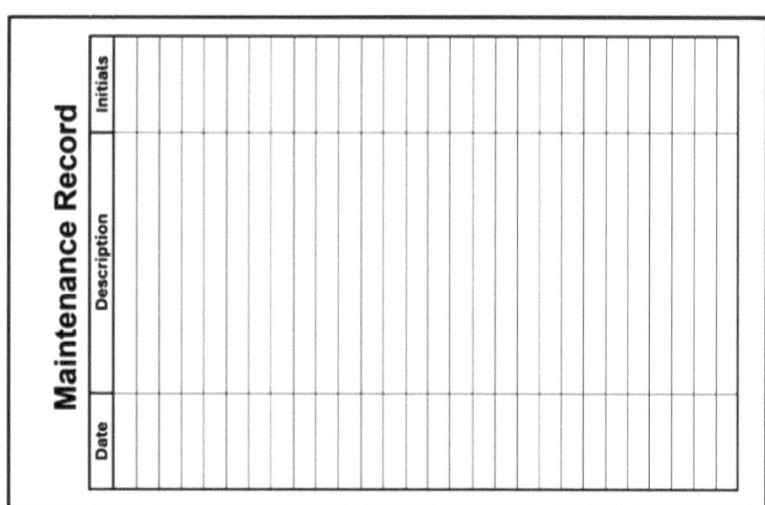

NON-HAZARDOUS WASTE

GENERATOR INFORMATION:

Company Name:	
Address:	
Phone #:	

CONTENTS:

NON-HAZARDOUS WASTE

HAZARDOUS WASTE

Federal law prohibits improper disposal.
If found, contact the nearest police or public safety authority or the US Environmental Protection Agency.

GENERATOR INFORMATION:

Company Name:	
Address:	
Phone #:	
Manifest Tracking #:	
Accumulation Start Date:	
EPA ID #:	
EPA Waste #:	

D.O.T. PROPER SHIPPING NAME

HAZARDOUS WASTE
HANDLE WITH CARE!

HAZCOM Secondary Labels

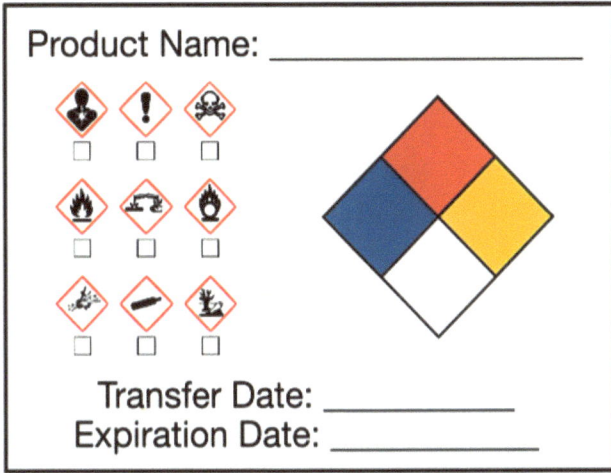
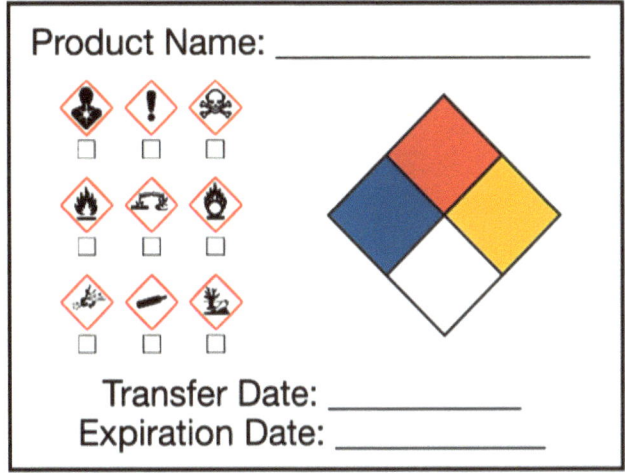
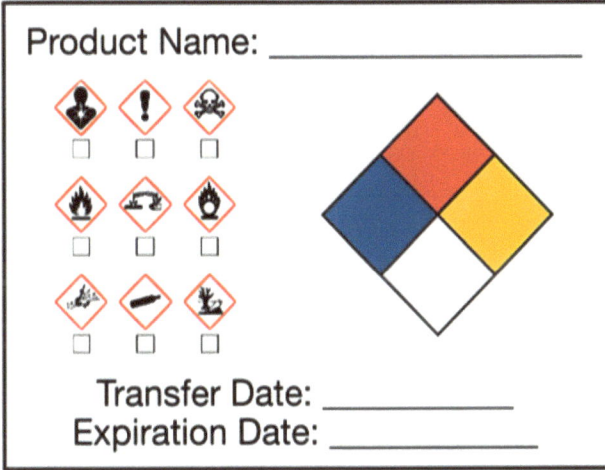
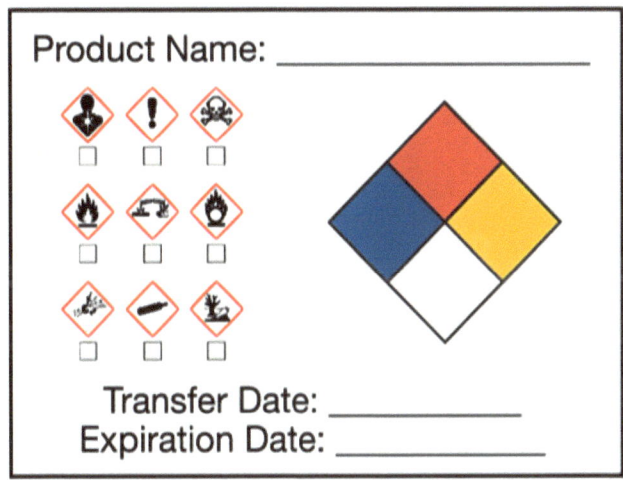
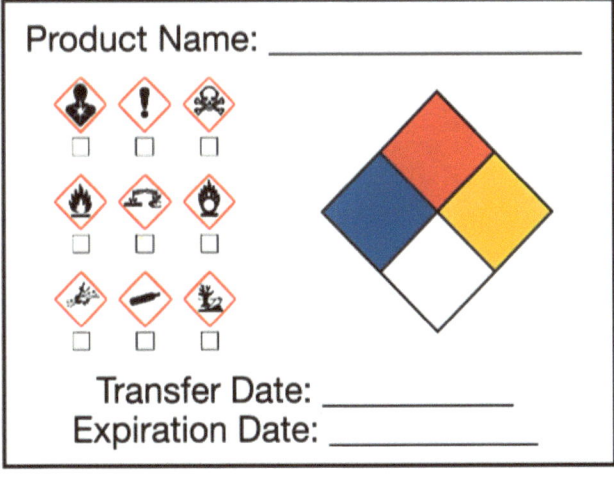
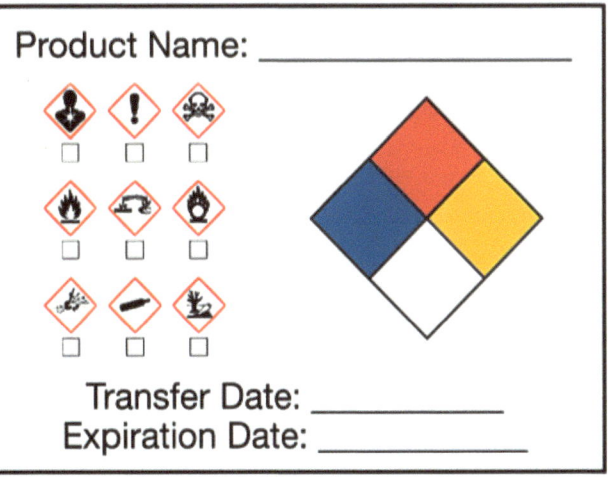

NFPA Diamond & GHS Pictograms

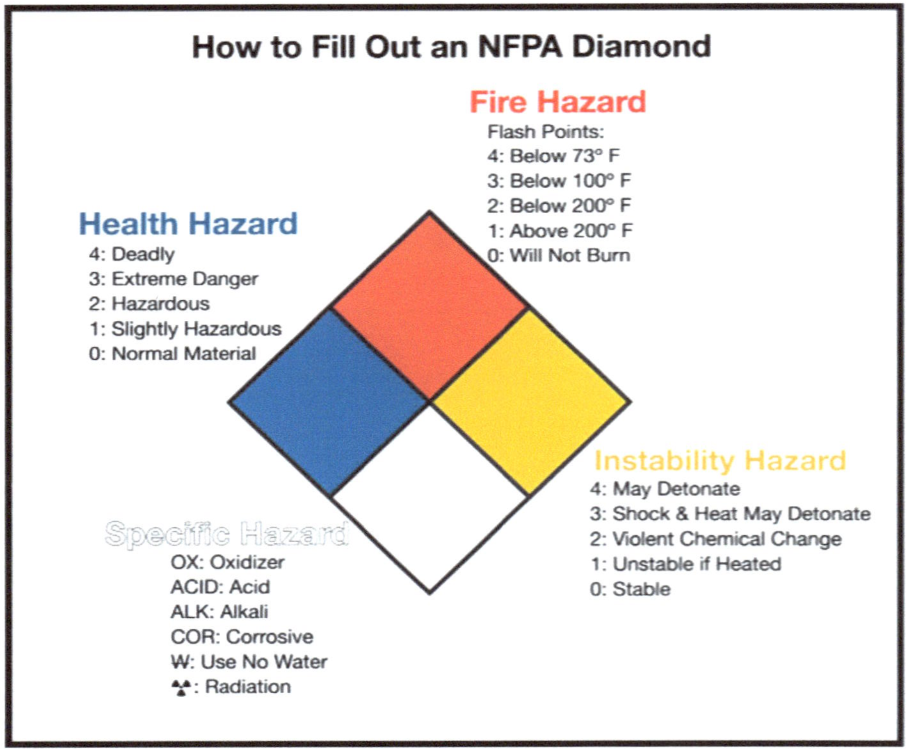

How to Fill Out an NFPA Diamond

Fire Hazard
Flash Points:
4: Below 73° F
3: Below 100° F
2: Below 200° F
1: Above 200° F
0: Will Not Burn

Instability Hazard
4: May Detonate
3: Shock & Heat May Detonate
2: Violent Chemical Change
1: Unstable if Heated
0: Stable

Health Hazard
4: Deadly
3: Extreme Danger
2: Hazardous
1: Slightly Hazardous
0: Normal Material

Specific Hazard
OX: Oxidizer
ACID: Acid
ALK: Alkali
COR: Corrosive
W: Use No Water
☢: Radiation

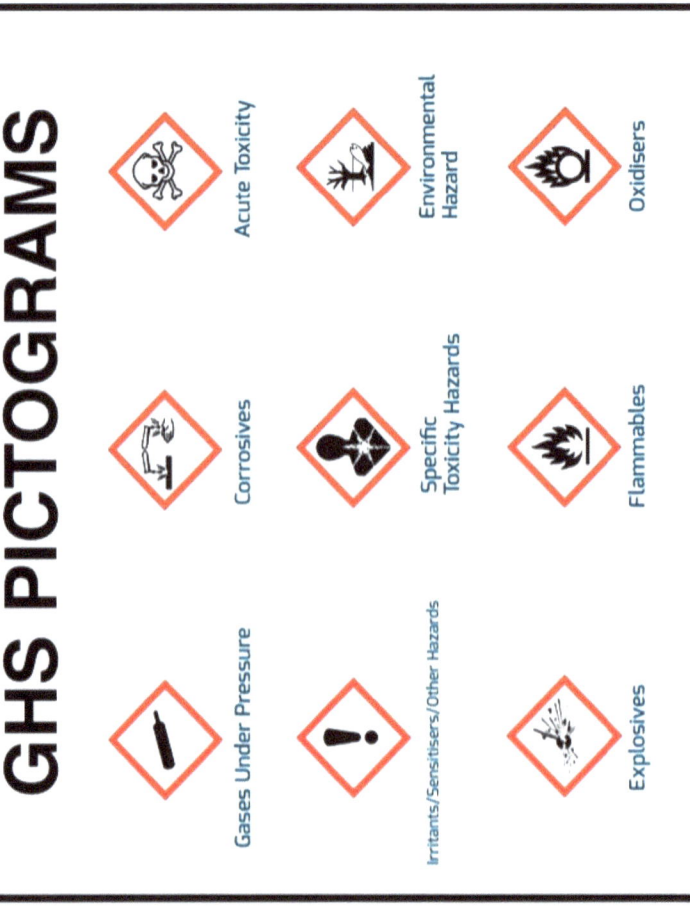

GHS PICTOGRAMS

- Gases Under Pressure
- Corrosives
- Acute Toxicity
- Irritants/Sensitisers/Other Hazards
- Specific Toxicity Hazards
- Environmental Hazard
- Explosives
- Flammables
- Oxidisers

Common Welding Symbols

Fillet Weld Location

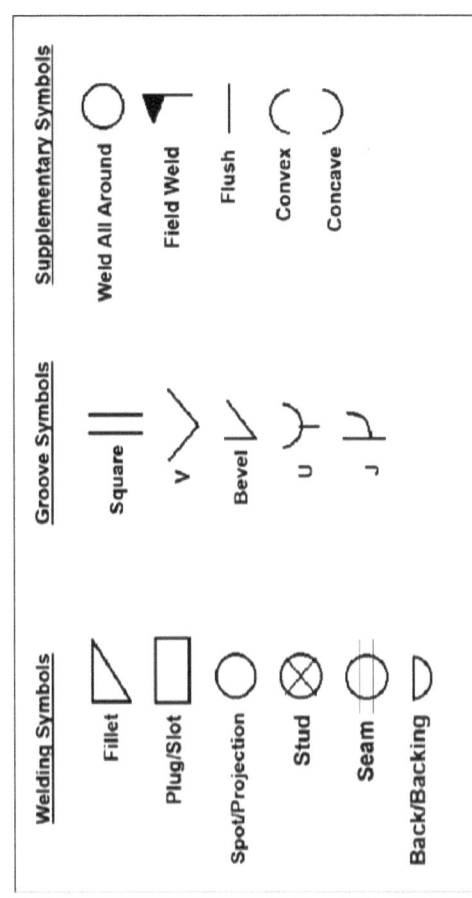

Welding Symbol Structure

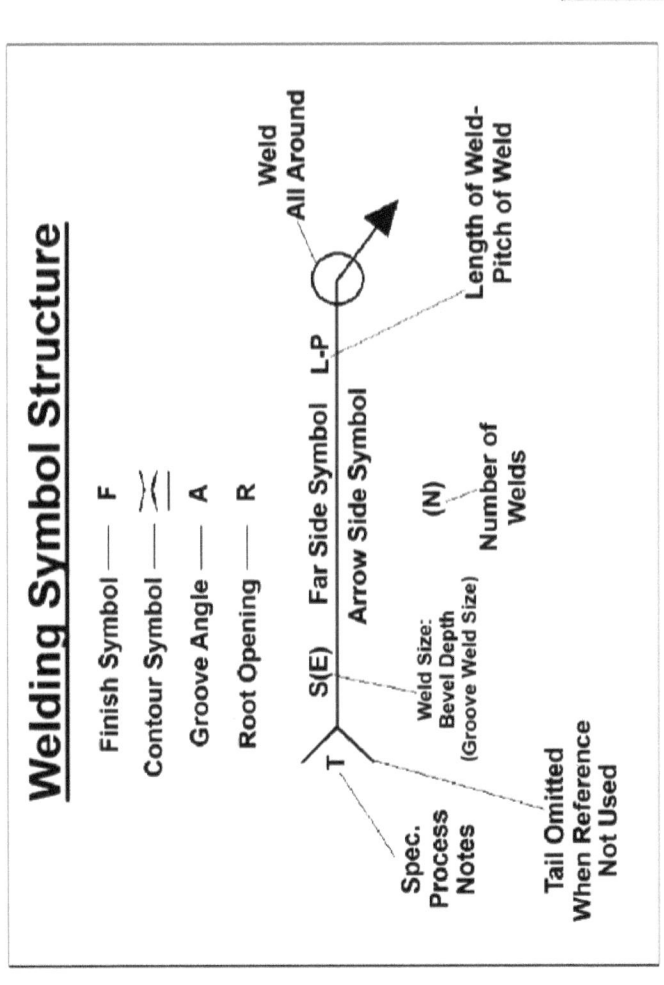

Reference: AWS A2.4-98, Standard Symbols for Welding, Brazing, and Nondestructive Examination

Common Plumbing Symbols

Pneumatically Operated Valve

Relief Valve

Centrifugal Pump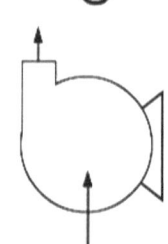

Rotary Pump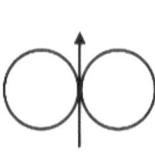

Pressure Gauge

Gate Valve

Globe Valve

Ball Valve

Butterfly Valve

Check Valve

Diaphragm Valve

Needle Valve

Common Electrical Symbols

Symbol	Name	Symbol	Name
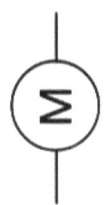	Outlet		Motor
	Normally Open Switch		Circuit Breaker
	Normally Closed Switch		Contactor
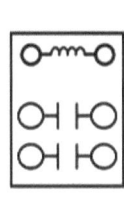	Fuse		Relay
	Fuse		Normally Open Contact
	Capacitor		Normally Closed Contact
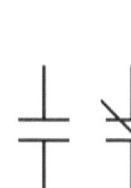	Transformer		Ground
	Fused Disconnect Switch		Coil
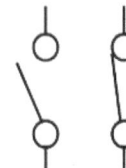	Battery		

Wire Gauge & Ampacity

18/5: Thermostat Wire

14 Gauge 15 Amps: Branch Circuits, Lighting Circuits

12 Gauge 20 Amps: Small Appliances, Kitchen & Bath Branch Circuits

10 Gauge 30 Amps: Appliances (HVAC, Water Heater, Dryer)

8 Gauge 40 Amps: Feeder & Large Appliance

6 Gauge 55 Amps: Feeder & Large Appliance

(LARGER SIZES WOULD BE FOR SERVICE ENTRANCE/FEEDER)

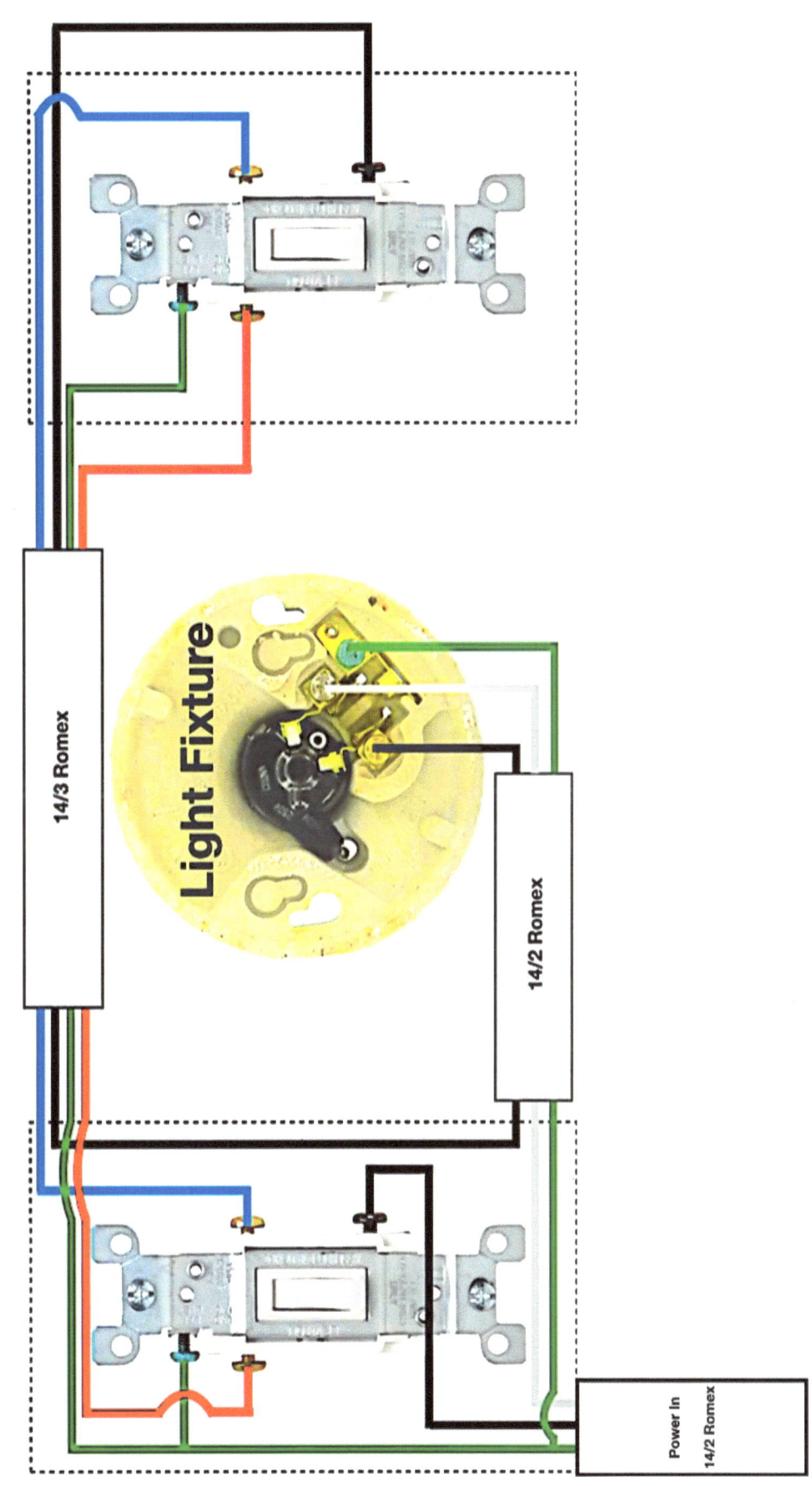

Receptacle & Plug Wiring

Duplex Receptacle, 5-15R, 15 Amp, 125 VAC

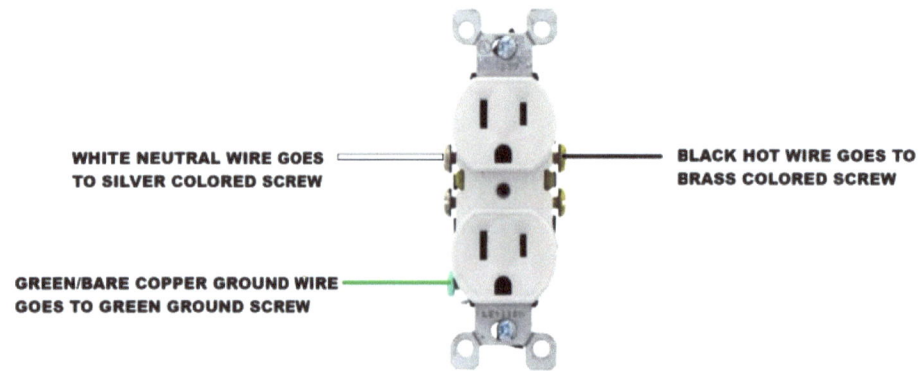

NEMA 5-20

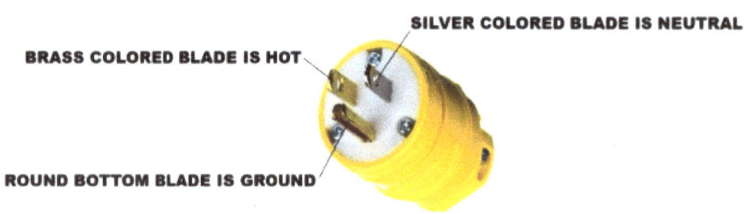

Polarized Cord, 2-Wire

Non-Polarized Cord, 2-Wire

Thermostat Wiring for a Furnace & Standard AC Unit

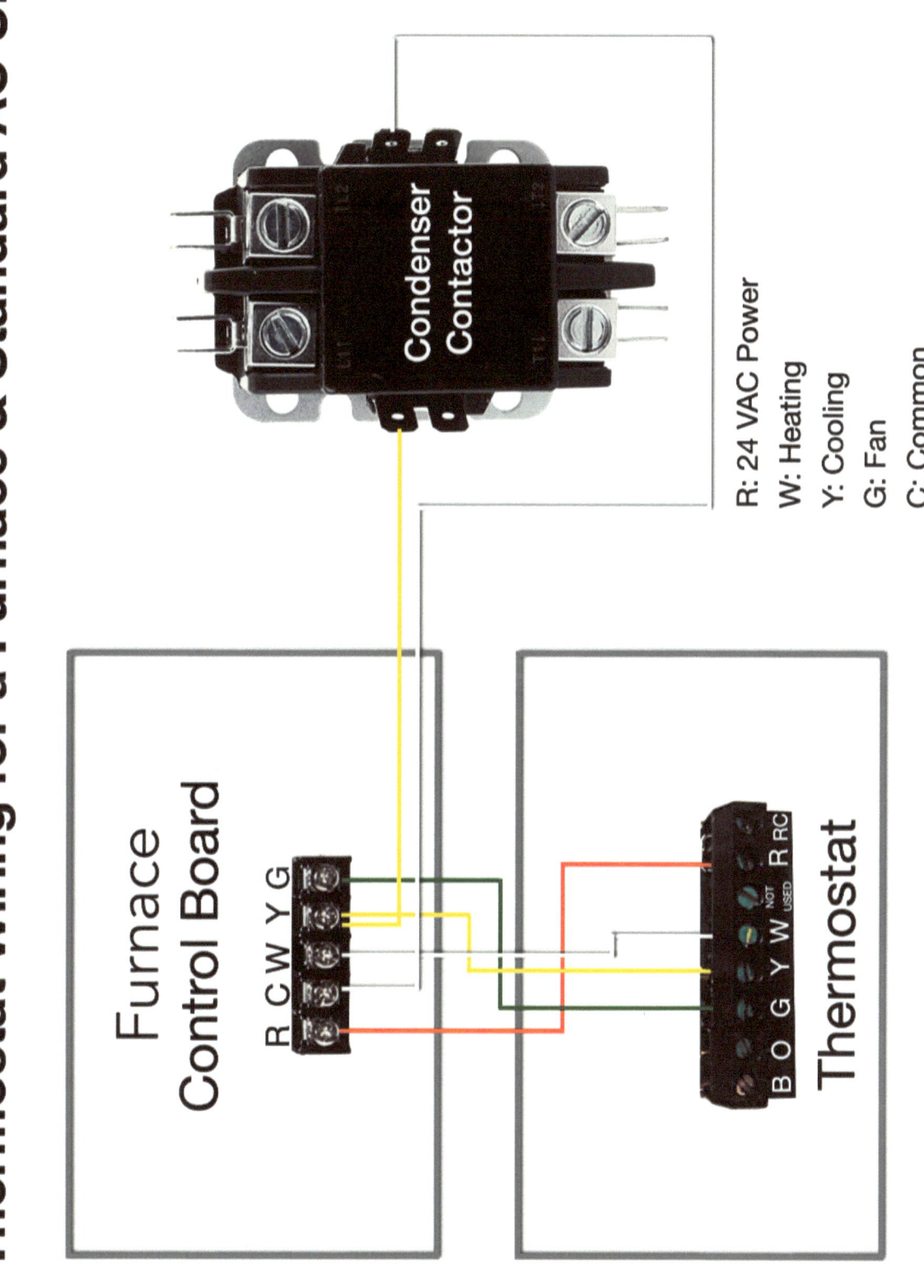

R: 24 VAC Power
W: Heating
Y: Cooling
G: Fan
C: Common

HVAC Refrigerant Circuit

1. Compressor
2. Discharge Line
3. Condenser
4. Condenser Cooling Fan
5. Liquid Line
6. Metering Device (Expansion Valve)
7. Expansion Line
8. Evaporator
9. Blower
10. Suction Line

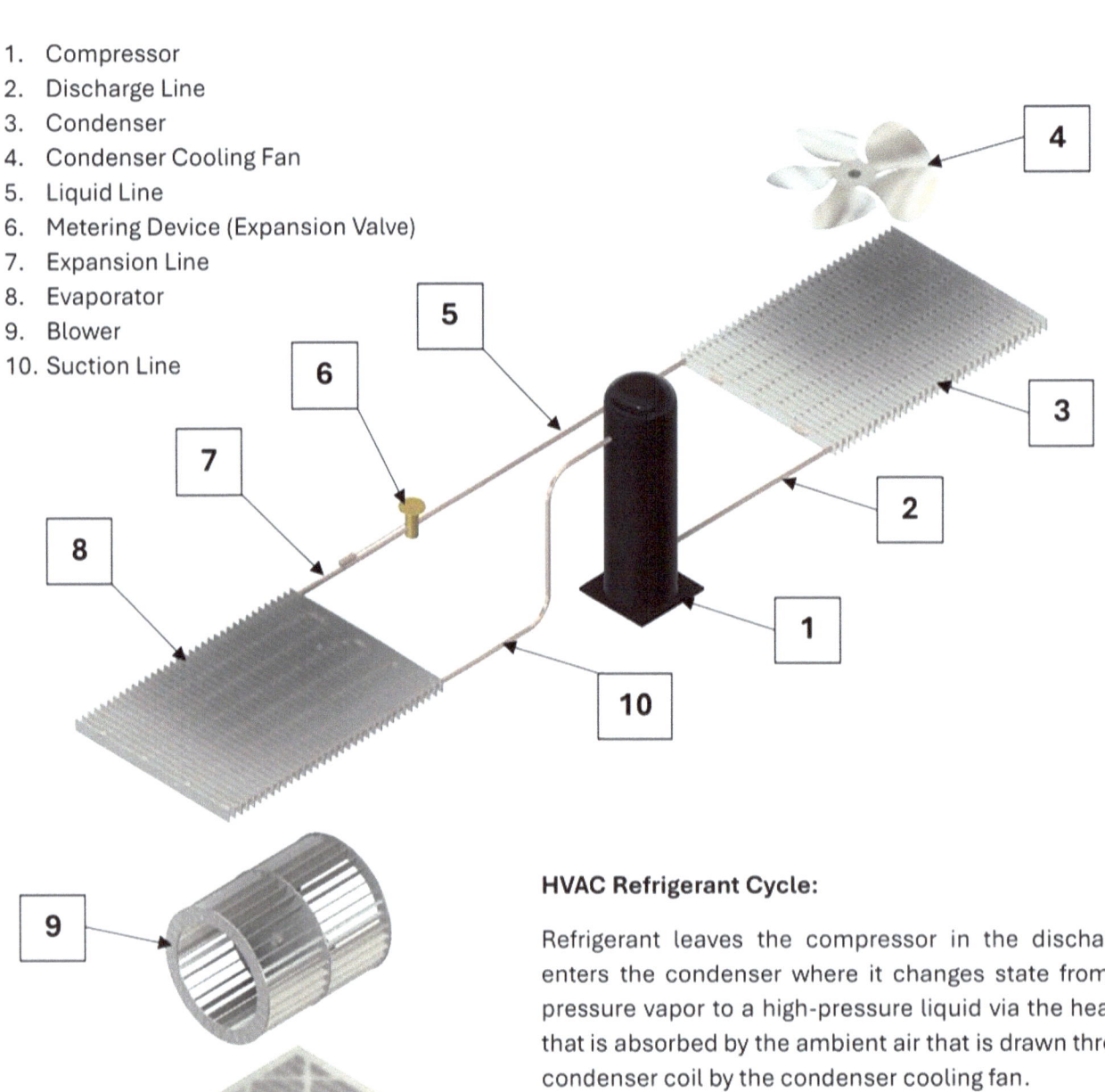

Air Filter

HVAC Refrigerant Cycle:

Refrigerant leaves the compressor in the discharge line, enters the condenser where it changes state from a high-pressure vapor to a high-pressure liquid via the heat energy that is absorbed by the ambient air that is drawn through the condenser coil by the condenser cooling fan.

Refrigerant then flows through the liquid line, into the metering device (expansion valve) were the refrigerant changes from a high-pressure liquid to a low-pressure liquid with some flash gas.

Refrigerant then flows into the evaporator via the expansion line, where it absorbs heat energy from the indoor air blowing across the evaporator coil. The refrigerant changes state to a vapor and leaves the evaporator in the suction line heading back to the compressor inlet.

Furnace Sequence of Operation

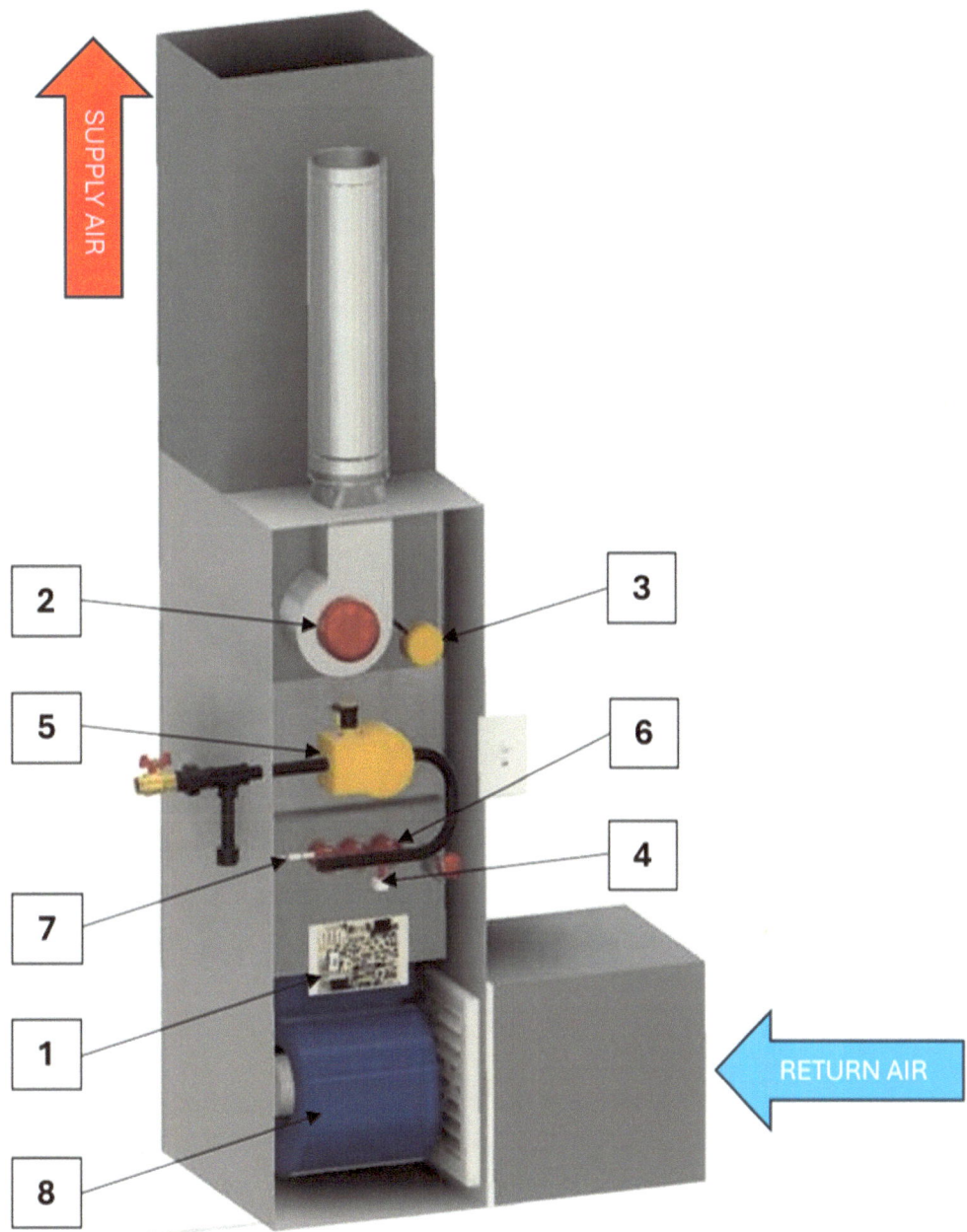

Sequence of Operation:

1. The thermostat calls for heat, sending 24 volts to the "W" terminal on the ignition control board.
2. The draft inducer fan starts.
3. The pressure switch closes.
4. The hot surface ignitor glows.
5. The gas valve opens. (3.5" W.C. is typical manifold gas pressure on a natural gas furnace.)
6. The burners ignite.
7. The flame sensing rod proves flame, via flame rectification.
8. The blower starts.

Troubleshooting Steps

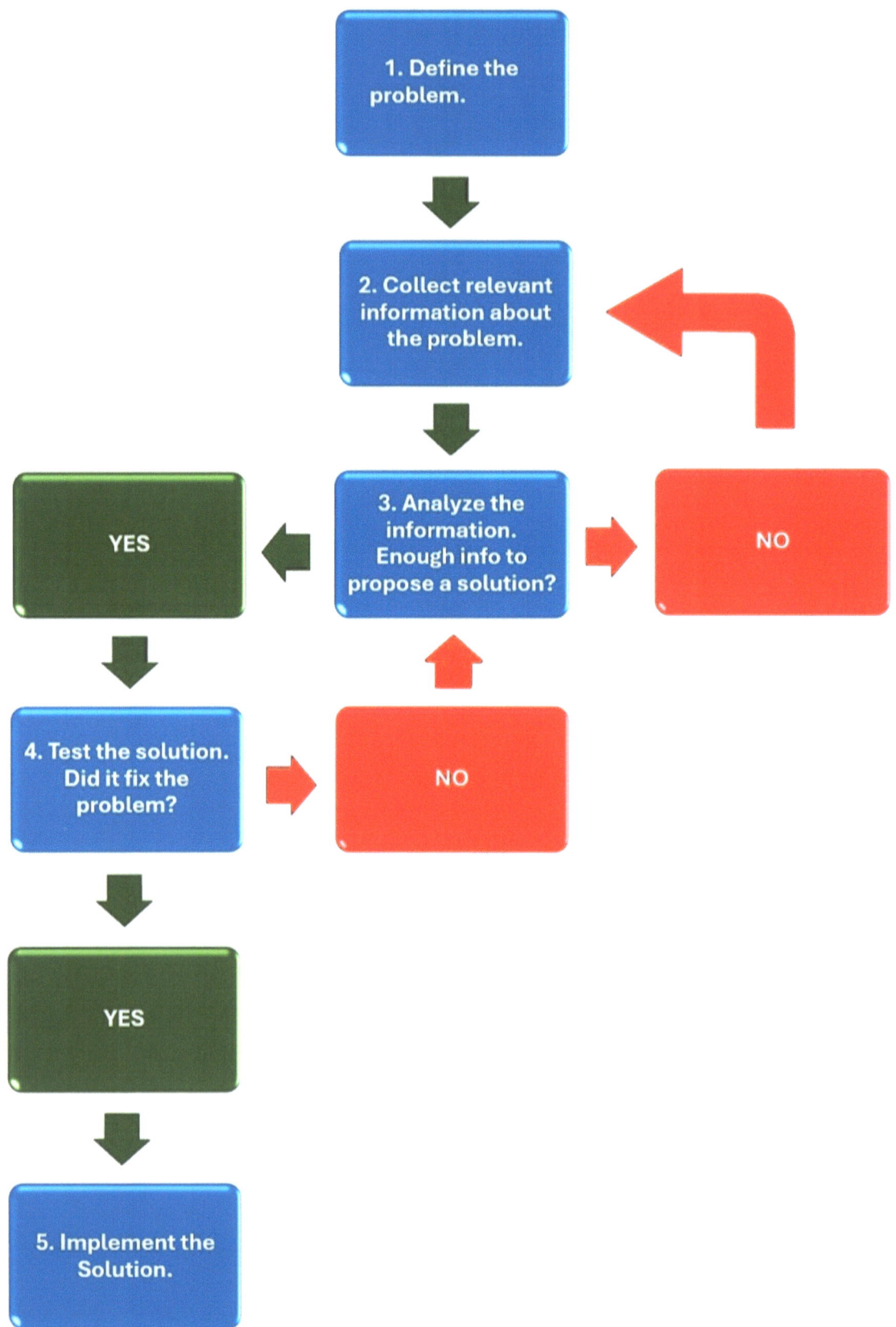

How to Reduce Waste in Your Facility

Reduce Wasted: Time, Materials, Labor, and Money

KAIZEN: A Japanese term meaning change for the better. Kaizen is a gradual, long-term approach to improve workflow and best business practice efficiency and quality. Needs management buy-in.

Kaizen is based on three principles:

1. Process & Results
2. Systemic Thinking
3. Non-Judgmental/Non-Blaming

Kaizen Cycle:

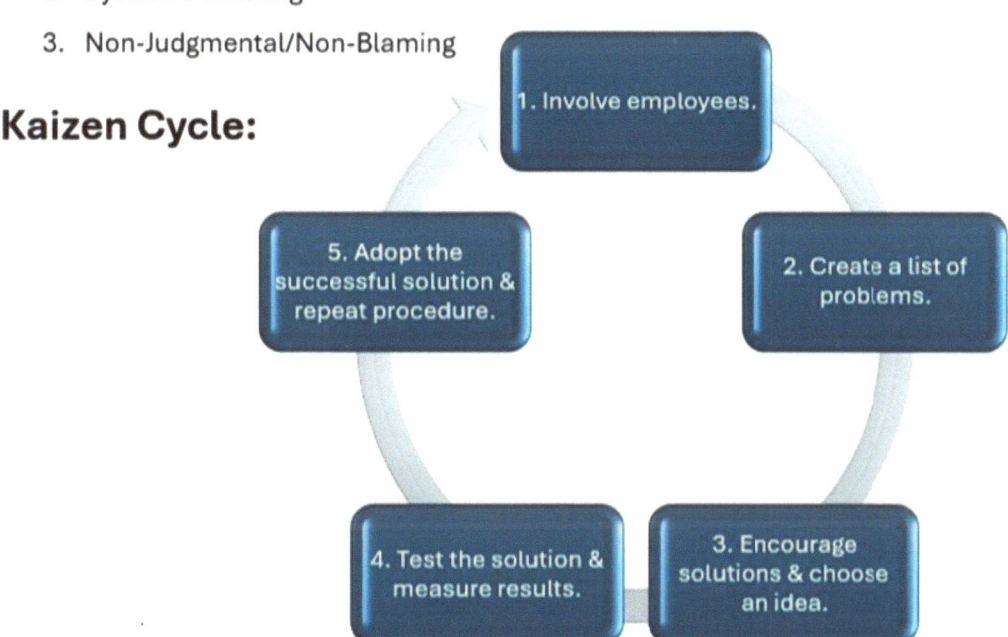

5S: 5S is a process for organizing your facility in an efficient, safe manner to increase productivity, reduce waste, and introduce standardized workflows. Needs management buy-in.

5S Process:

1. Siri: Sort, Clearing, Classify

2. Seiton: Straighten, Simplify, Set in Order, Configure

3. Seiso: Sweep, Shine, Scrub, Clean & Check

4. Seiketsu: Standardize, Stabilize, Conformity

5. Shitsuke: Sustain, Self-Discipline, Standardization

Weights, Measures, Formulas

1 Inch =	2.540 Centimeters	25.4 Millimeters
1 Foot =	30.48 Centimeters	304.8 Millimeters
1 Yard =	91.44 Centimeters	914.4 Millimeters
1 Centimeter =	.3937 Inches	10 Millimeters
1 Millimeter =	.03937 Inches	0.1 Centimeters
1 Cu. Foot =	1,728 Cu. Inches	
1 Cu. Foot =	7.48 Gallons	
1 (US) Gallon =	231 Cu. Inches of Water	
1 Gallon of Water =	8.34 LBS.	
1 Liquid Gallon =	4 Quarts	
1 Dry Quart =	2 Pints	
1 Pound =	16 Ounces	
1 Ton =	2,000 LBS	
1 (US) Pint =	16 Fl. Ounces	
1 Cup =	8 Fl. Ounces	
1 Tablespoon =	0.5 Fl. Ounces	
1 Teaspoon =	0.16 Fl. Ounces	
1 Metric Ton =	2,204.6223 Pounds	
1 Centiliter =	10 Milliliters	0.338 Fl. Ounces
1 Deciliter =	10 Centiliters	3.38 Fl. Ounces
1 Liter =	10 deciliters	33.8 Fl. Ounces
1 Cu. Meter =	1,000 Cu. Decimeters	35.31467 Cu. Yards
1 Cu. Centimeter of Water =	1 Gram	
1 Cu. Meter =	1,000 Liters	1 Metric Ton
1 BTU Raises 1 LB of Water =	1° Fahrenheit	
12,000 BTU's =	1 Ton	

Ohm's Law Formulas:

Amps(I) = Volts/Resistance

Resistance(R)Ω = Volts/Amps

Volts(E) = Amps x Resistance

Watts(P) = Amps x Volts

Horsepower Formulas:

DC Horsepower = Volts x Amps x Efficiency/746

1PH AC Horsepower = Volts x Amps x Efficiency x Power Factor/746

3PH AC Horsepower = Volts x Amps x Efficiency x Power Factor x 1.73/746

Chain & Sling Storage Rack

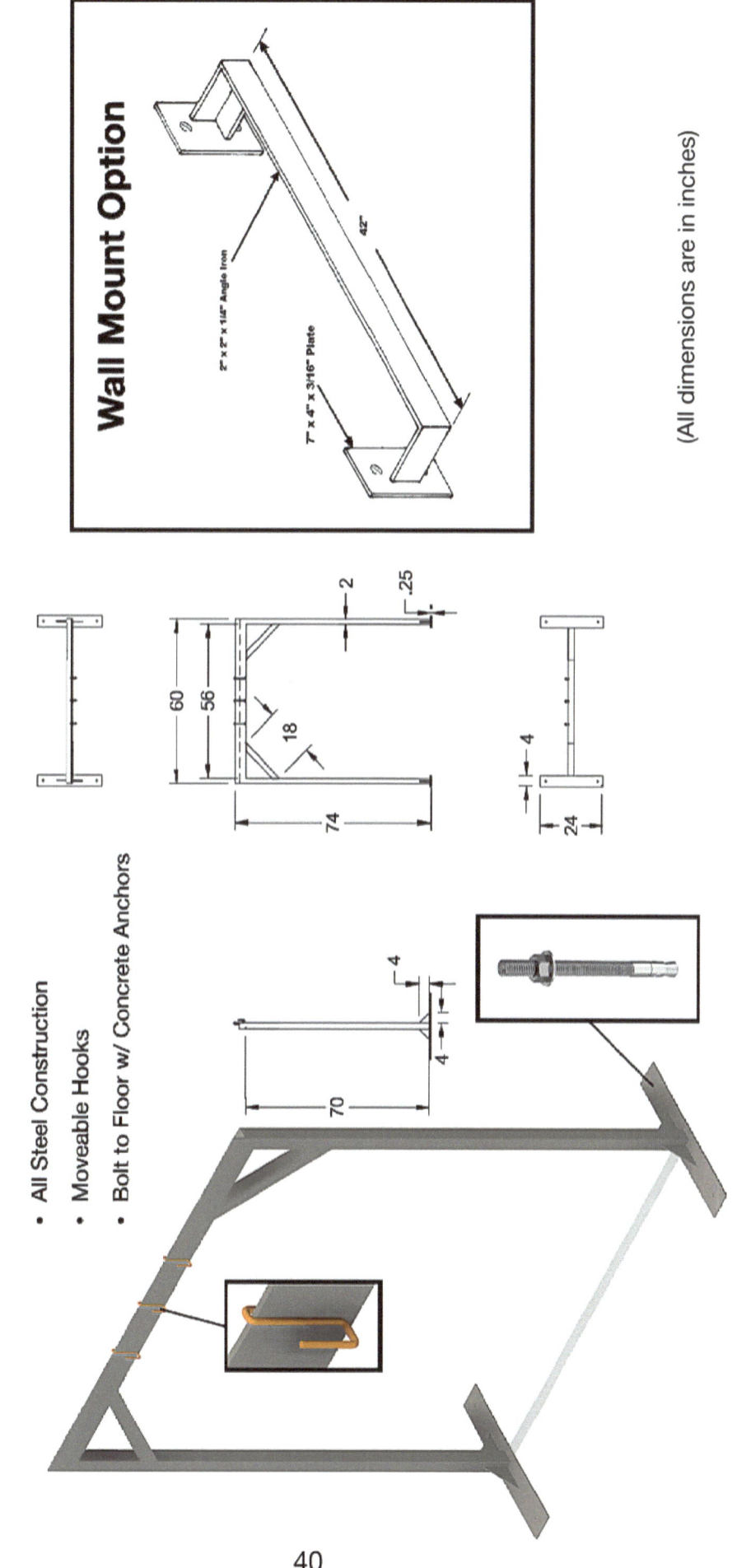

Wall Mount Option

- All Steel Construction
- Moveable Hooks
- Bolt to Floor w/ Concrete Anchors

(All dimensions are in inches)

Parts Rack

- All Steel Construction
- 3-Tiers
- 3/4" #9 Expanded Steel Shelves

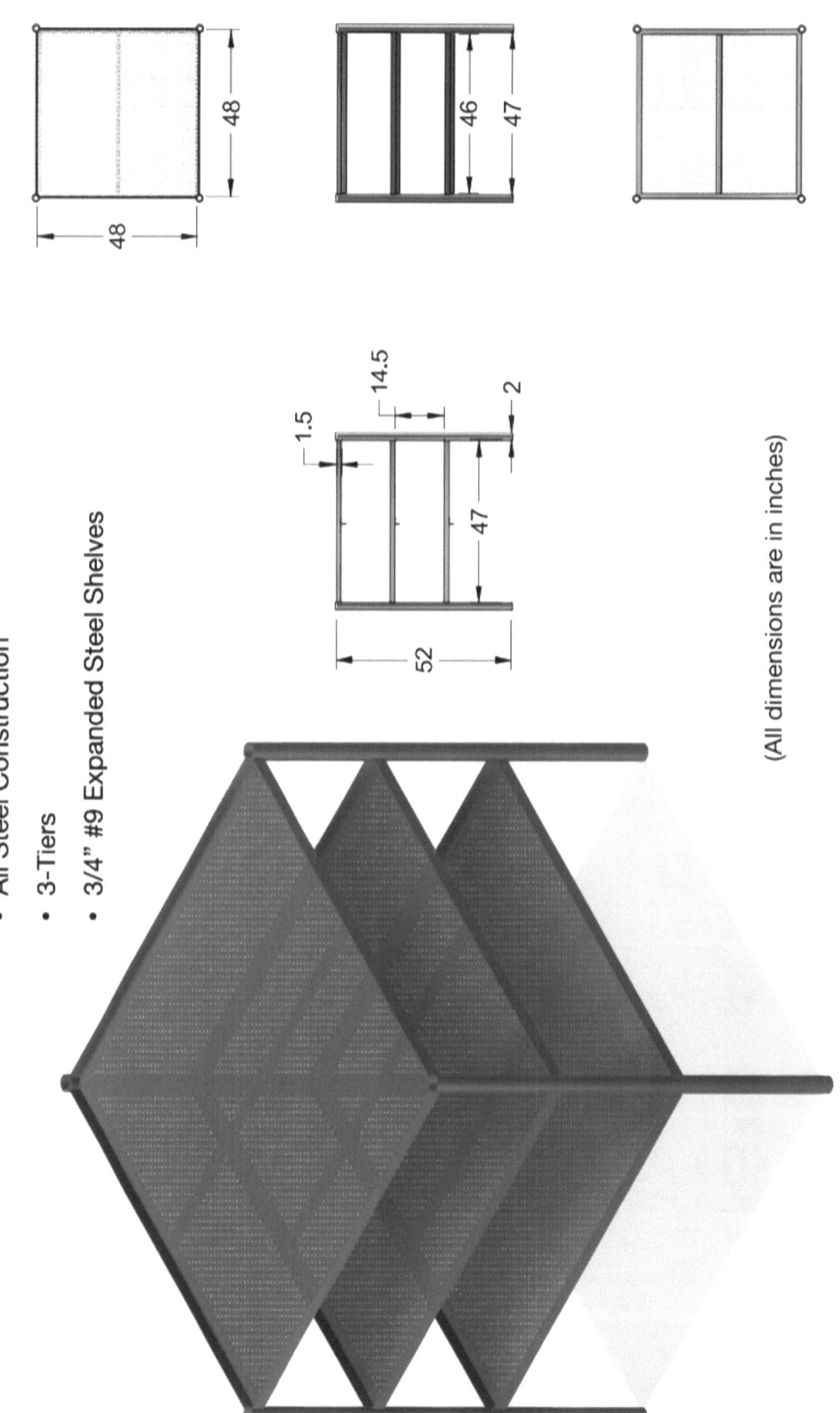

(All dimensions are in inches)

Work Bench

- 4" Heavy-Duty Swivel Casters
- All Steel Construction

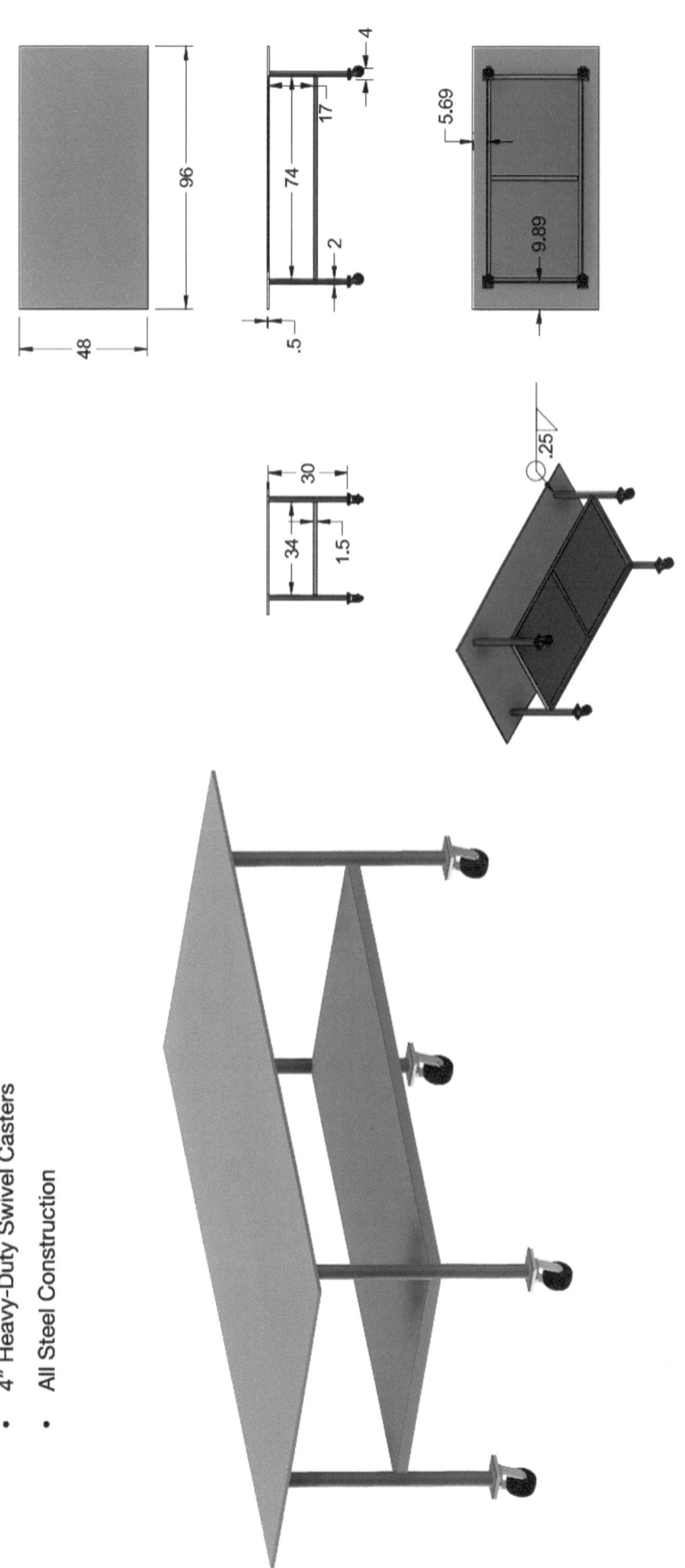

Kidney-Loop Filtration & Transfer Cart

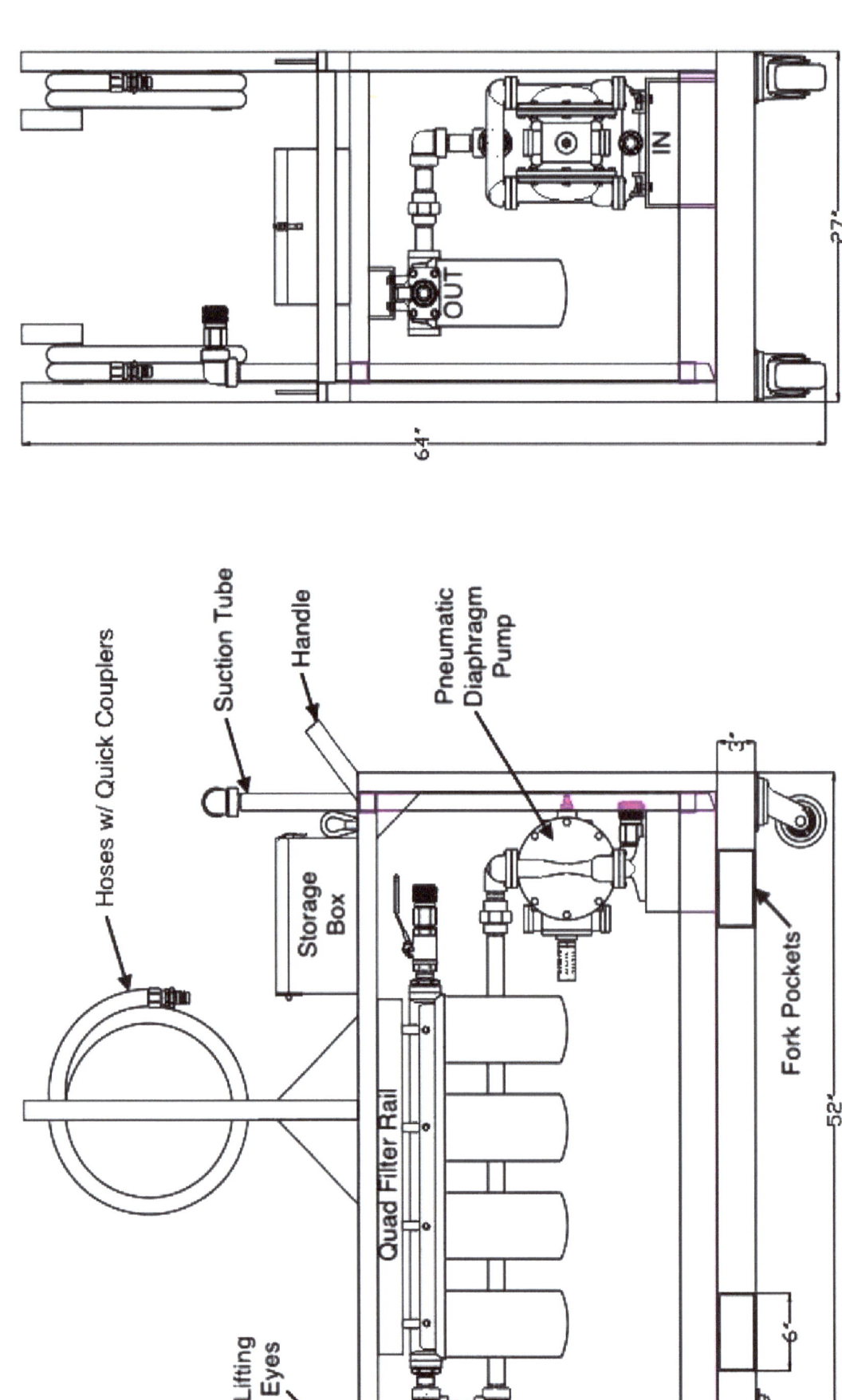

Self-Dumping Hopper

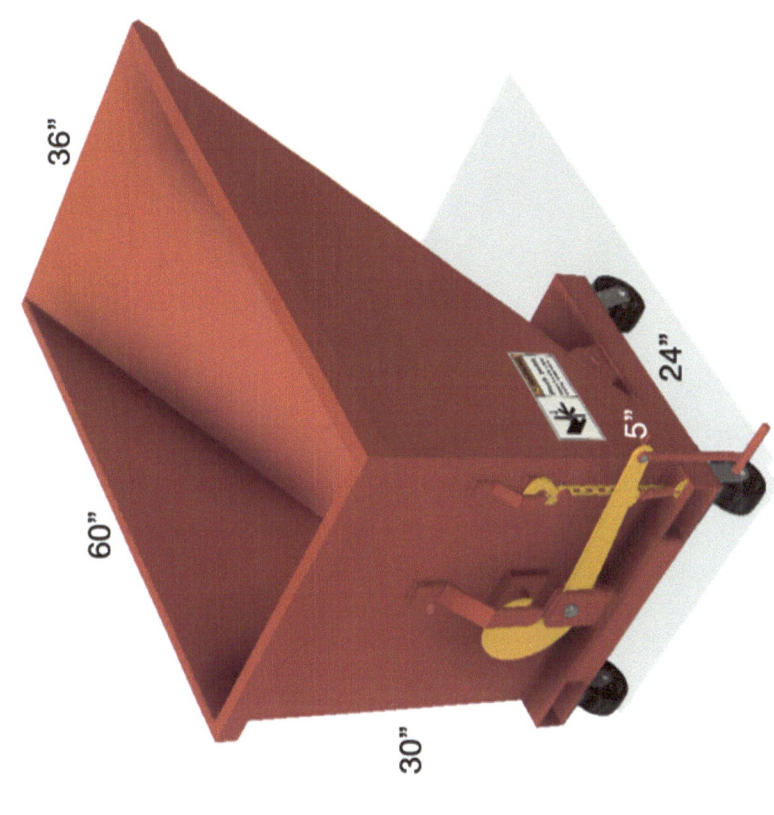

- Rectangular Tube Forklift Base: 3" x 5" x 0.12" Carbon Steel Rectangle Tube A500/A513 Hot Rolled
- 1/8" Thick Steel Hopper Construction
- Safety Chain w/Clasp
- Spring Return Hopper Release T-Handle
- 2" x 1" Rectangular Tubing Reinforced Top Hopper Edge
- Heavy-Duty Casters
- Pinch Point Warning Decals

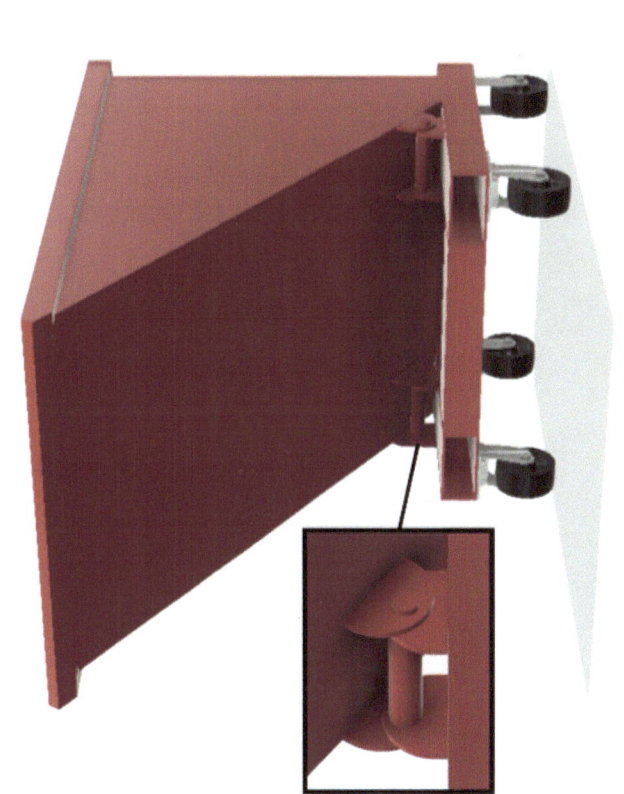

Spool Storage Rack

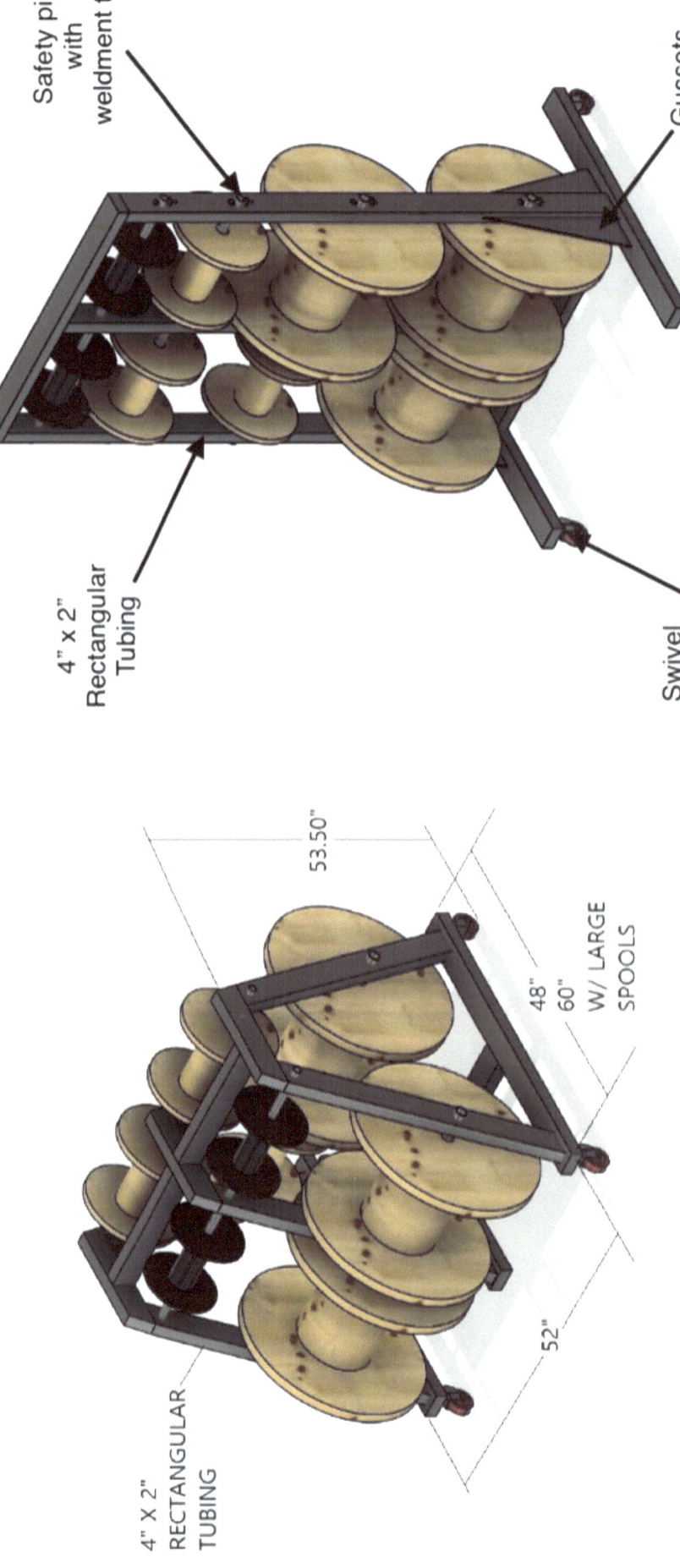

- All Steel Construction
- Store: Wire, Rope, Tubing, Cable, Etc.

55-Gal Drum Lube Cart

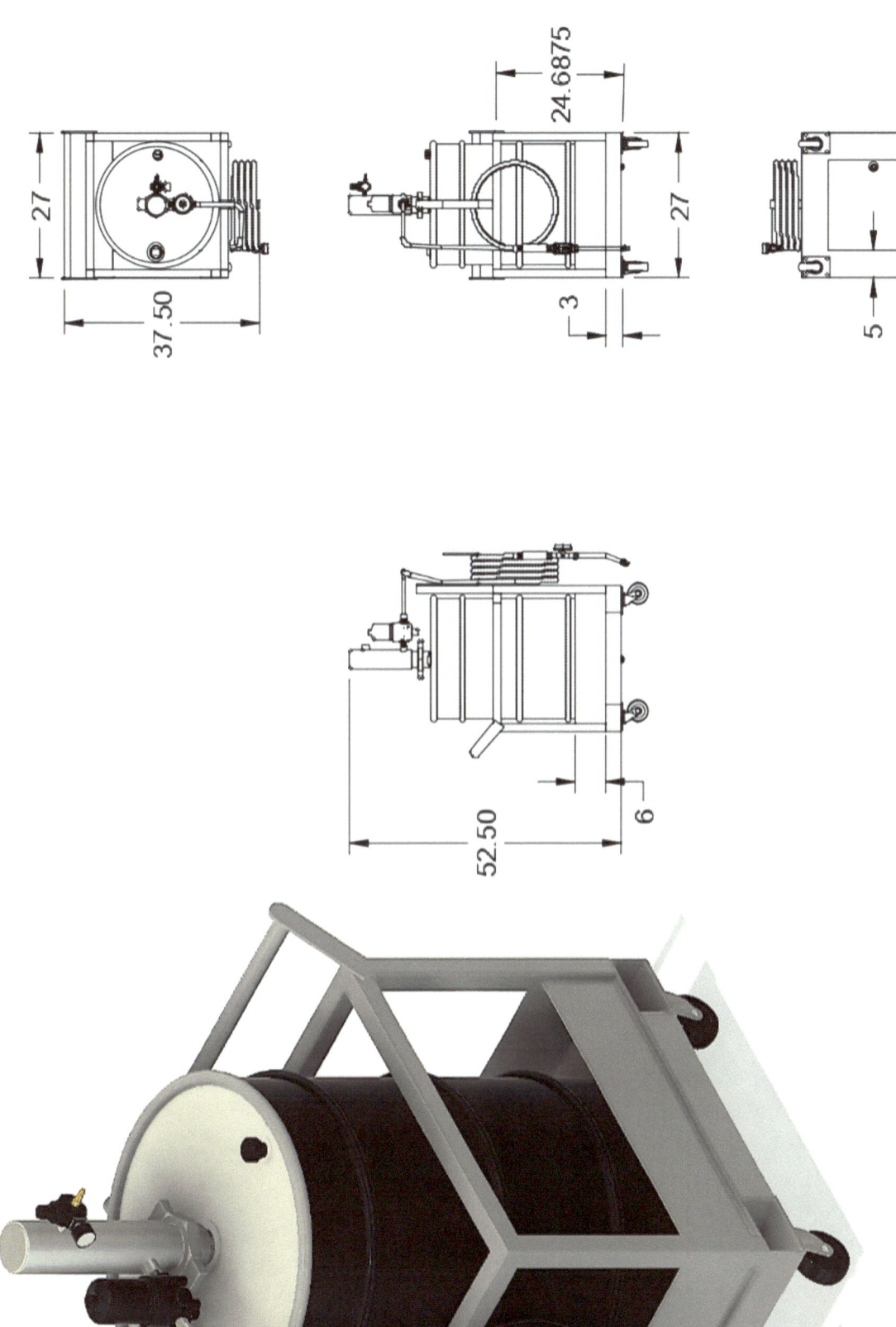

Hydroelectric Oil Filter Crusher:

The oil squeezed out of the drained, crushed oil filters can be recycled, and the oil filter canisters can often times be recycled as scrap metal. By utilizing an oil filter crusher in your facility, you can reduce storage space and reduce the waste stream of used oil filters in your facility, saving money.

Absorbent Pad Wringer:

The oil squeezed out of used absorbent pads can be recycled, and the used absorbent pads can often times be used again. By utilizing an absorbent pad wringer in your facility, you can reduce storage space and reduce the waste stream of used absorbent pads in your facility, saving money.

Absorbent pad wringers can sit on an oil drain table, or clamp to a 55-gallon drum.

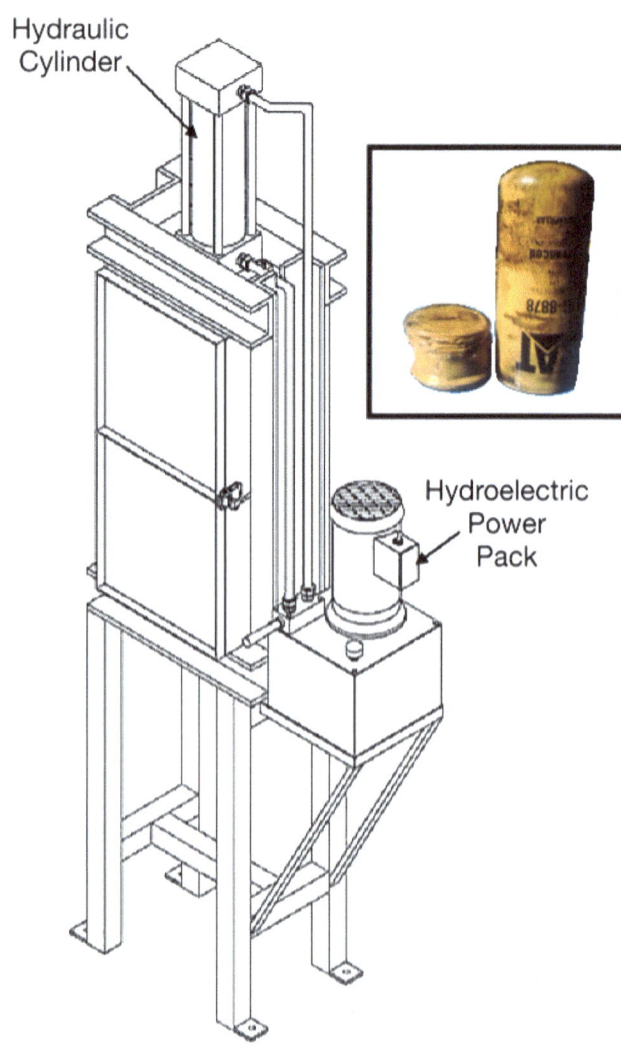
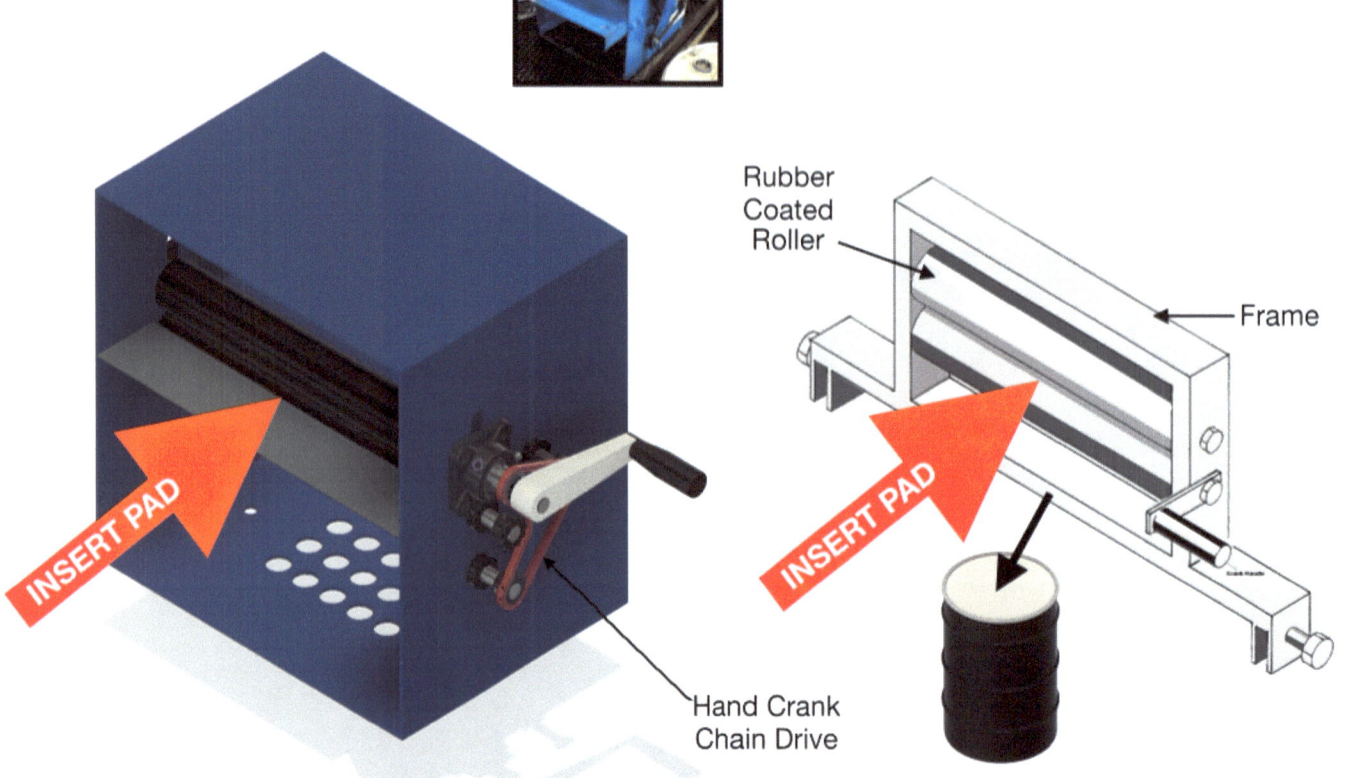

Aerosol Can Recycle System

"...a steel aerosol can that does not contain a significant amount of liquid (e.g., a can that has been punctured and drained) would meet the definition of scrap metal (40 CFR 261.1 (c) (6)), and, if it is to be recycled, would be exempt from regulation under 40 CFR 261.6 (a) (3) (iv)."

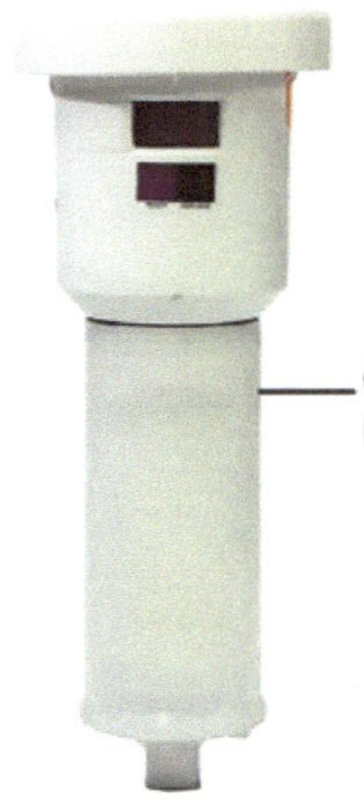

Coalescing/Carbon Filter/Breather

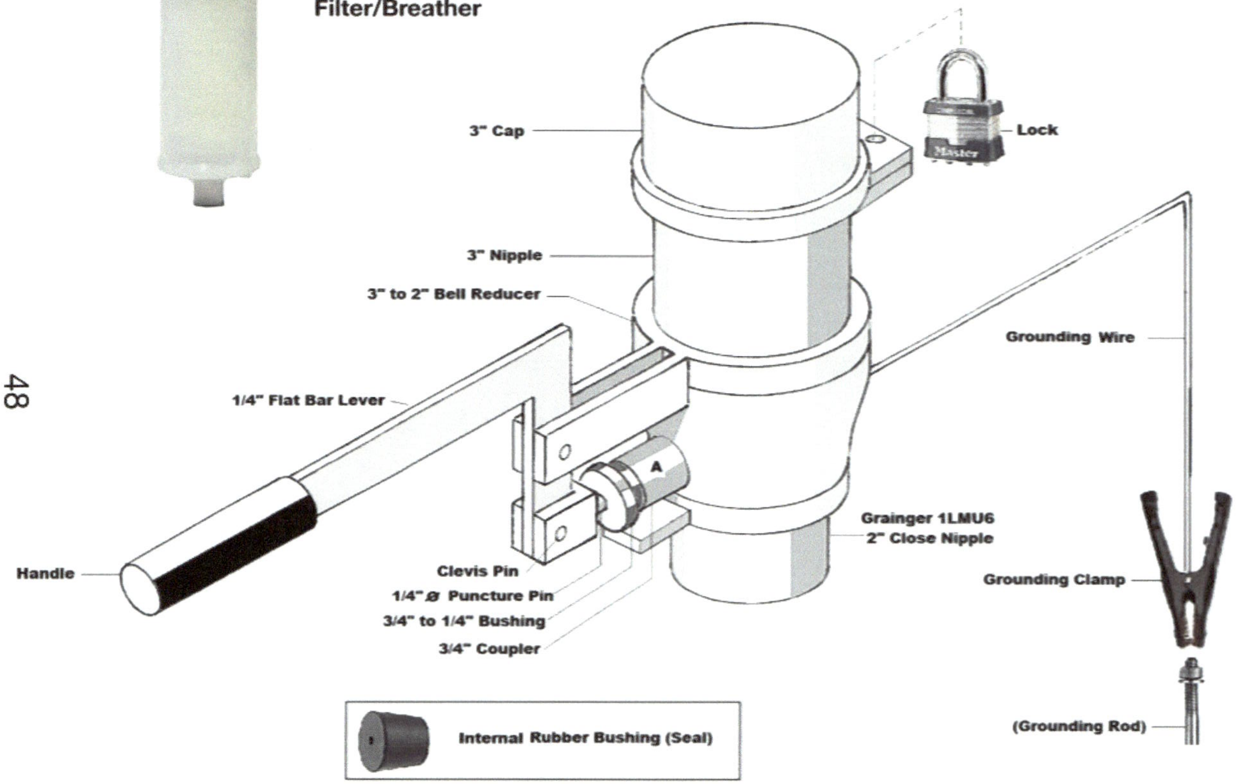

- 3" Cap
- 3" Nipple
- 3" to 2" Bell Reducer
- 1/4" Flat Bar Lever
- Handle
- Lock
- Clevis Pin
- 1/4" Ø Puncture Pin
- 3/4" to 1/4" Bushing
- 3/4" Coupler
- Grainger 1LMU6 2" Close Nipple
- Grounding Wire
- Grounding Clamp
- (Grounding Rod)
- Internal Rubber Bushing (Seal)
- Detail-A

An aerosol can recycle system is designed to safely puncture empty aerosol cans so they can be reclassified as scrap metal. The puncture device screws into a 2" bung on a 55-gallon drum. The coalescing/carbon filter screws into the 3/4" bung.

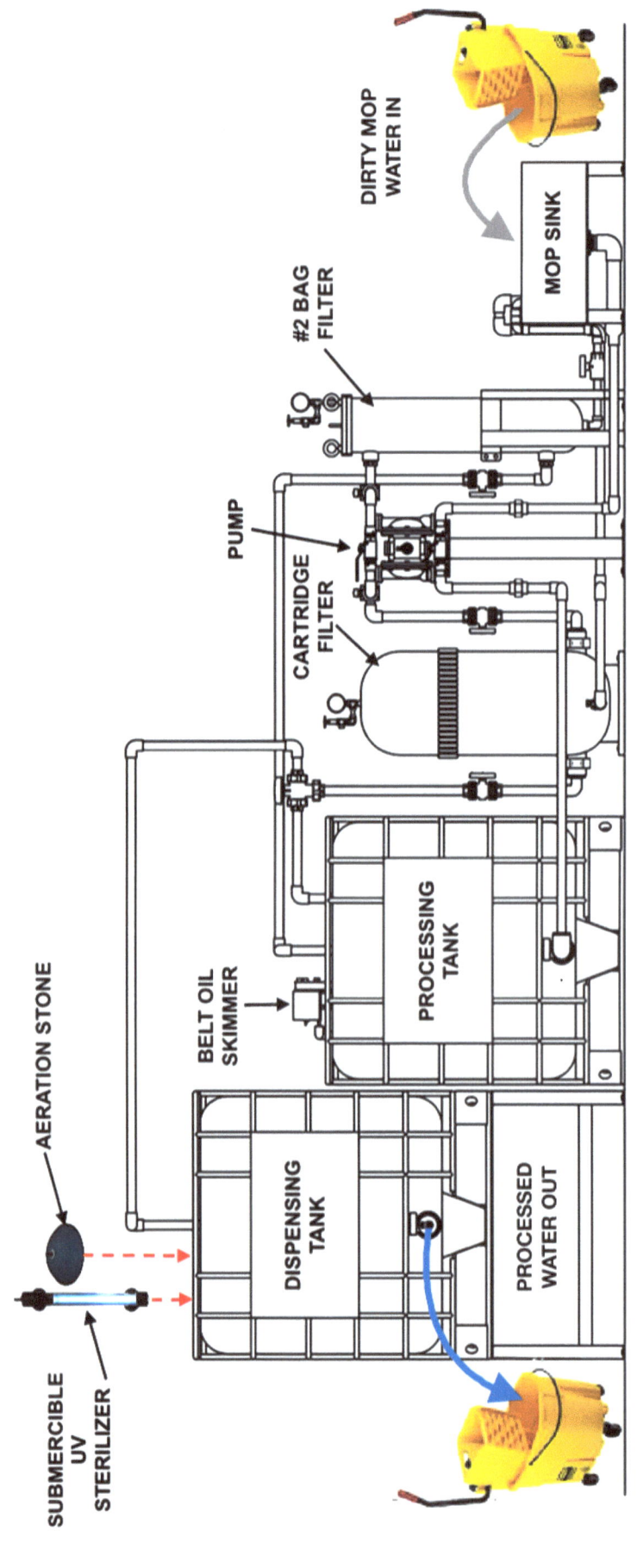

Belt-Type Oil Skimmer:

A belt-type oil skimmer uses a motor driven oleophilic belt to slowly skim oil contamination off the surface of a body of water or coolant sump on a piece of equipment. The oil sticks to the belt and gets scraped off inside the oil skimmer. The collected oil can be recycled. Belt-type oil skimmers are great for applications where the water level stays consistent.

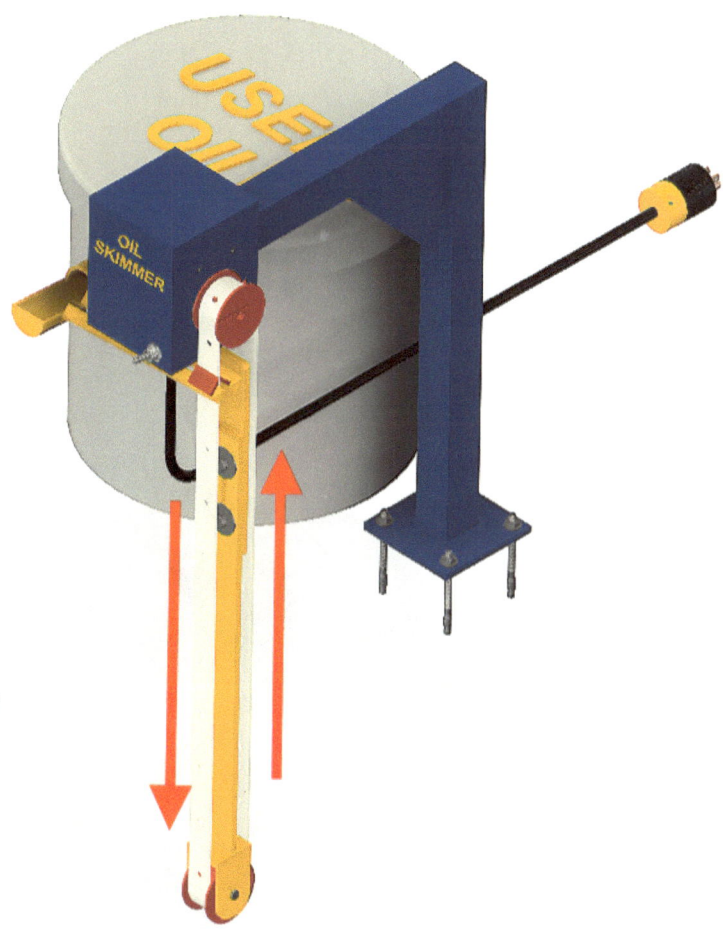

120 VAC Gear Motor

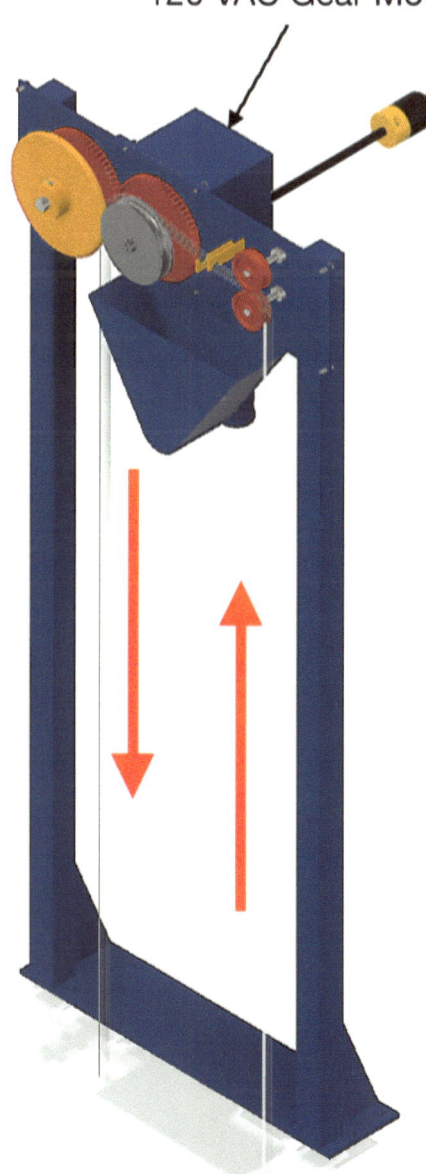

Tube-Type Oil Skimmer:

A tube-type oil skimmer uses a motor driven oleophilic tube to slowly skim oil contamination off the surface of a body of water, or coolant sump on a piece of equipment. The oil sticks to the tube and get scraped off inside the oil skimmer. The collected oil can be recycled. Tube-type oil skimmers are great for applications where the water level rises & falls often.

Other Types of Oil Skimmers:
- Drum
- Mop
- Rope
- Weir
- Disc
- Pipe

Mobile Oil Drain Pan:
This mobile drain pan is constructed of 1/8" steel with a 3/4" #9 expanded metal grate on top. Collected oil can be pumped out, or drained out. It's low profile design allows it to fit under a piece of equipment easily.

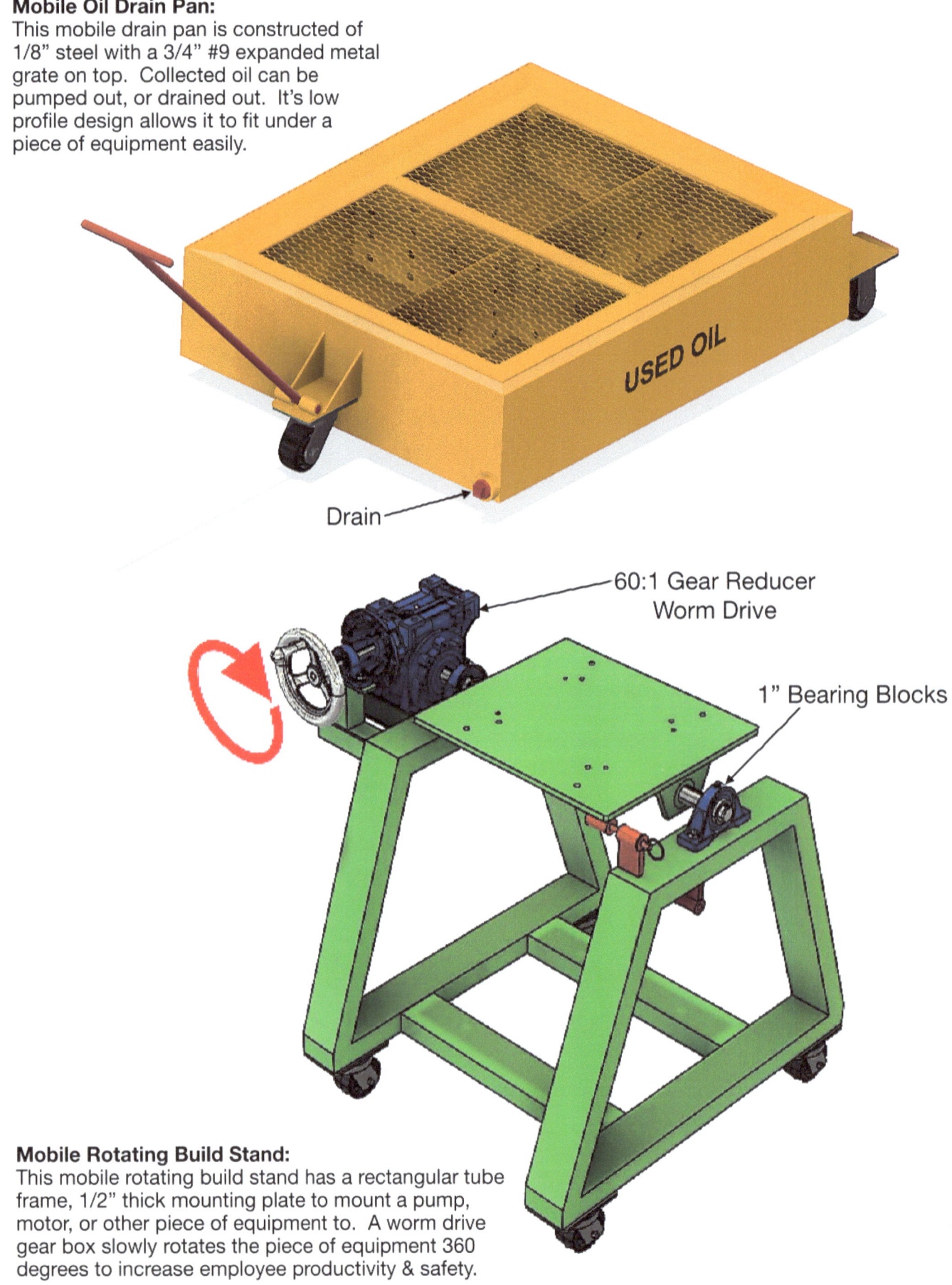

Mobile Rotating Build Stand:
This mobile rotating build stand has a rectangular tube frame, 1/2" thick mounting plate to mount a pump, motor, or other piece of equipment to. A worm drive gear box slowly rotates the piece of equipment 360 degrees to increase employee productivity & safety.

Stationary Oil Reclaim System

NOTES:

- SYSTEM CONSISTS OF TWO TANKS, TWO PUMPS, TWO FILTER HOUSINGS, FRAME, ALL GROUNDED.
- PROCESS LINES WILL BE MADE OF $3/16$ STAINLESS STEEL TUBING.
- PROCESS CONNECTIONS WILL BE STAINLESS STEEL SWAGE LOCK FITTINGS & BALL VALVES.
- REMOVABLE POLY PRO DRIP PAN WILL SIT ON BOTTOM SHELF W/ INTEGRATED $1/2$" DRAIN VALVE. 43.75" x 17" x 2"
- 1.50" SQUARE TUBE FRAME

(Grounding wire to prevent static charge buildup. Should be attached to metal structure of building)

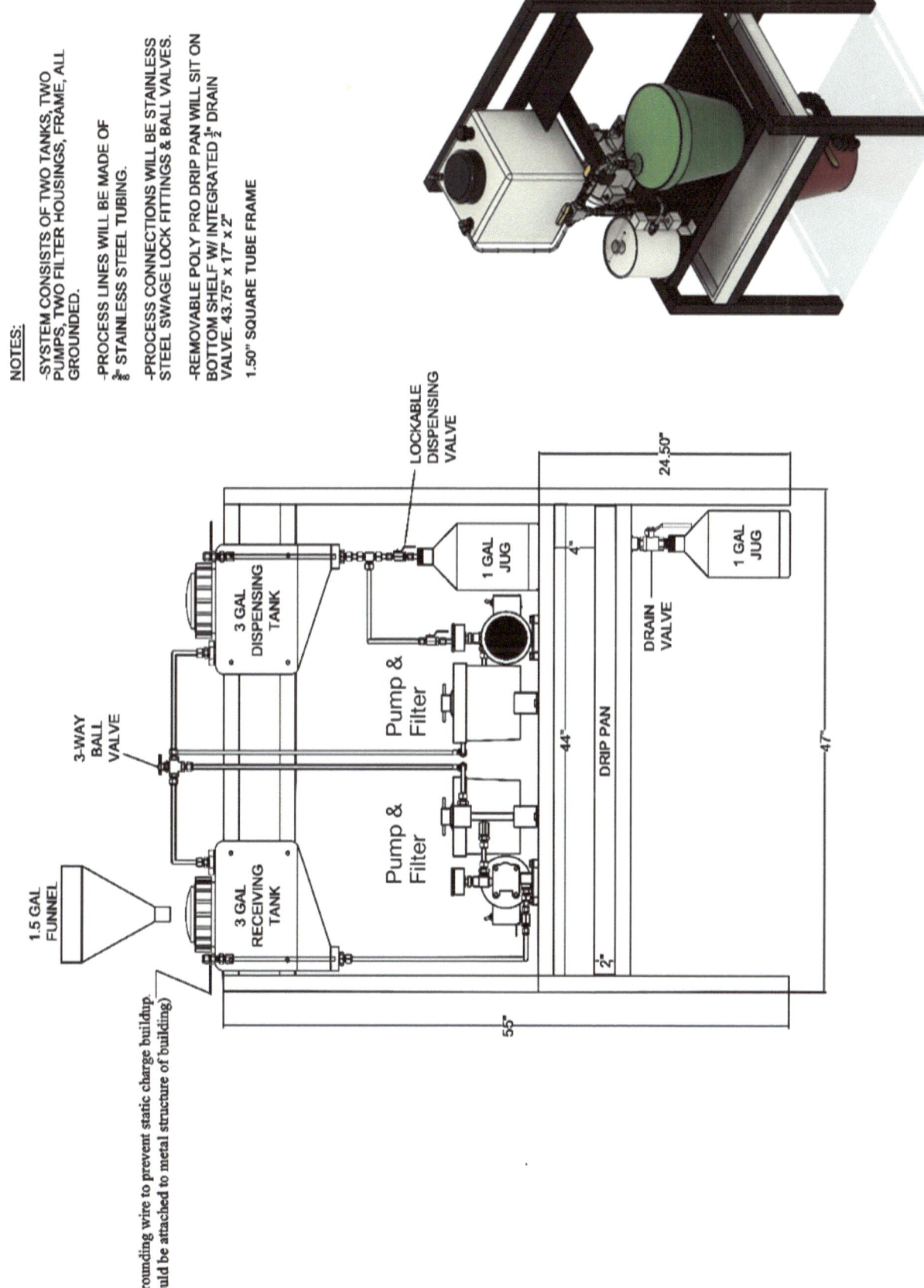

Inches to Millimeters

Fraction	Decimal	Millimeters
1/64"	.015625	.3969
1/32"	.03125	.7938
1/16"	.0625	1.5875
3/32"	.09375	2.3813
7/64"	.109375	2.7781
1/8"	.125	3.1750
5/32"	.15625	3.9688
11/64"	.171875	4.3656
3/16"	.1875	4.7625
7/32"	.21875	5.556
1/4"	.25	6.3500
9/32"	.28125	7.1438
5/16"	.3125	7.9375
11/32"	.34375	8.7313
3/8"	.375	9.5250
13/32"	.40625	10.3188
7/16"	.4375	11.1125
15/32"	.46875	11.9063
1/2"	.50	12.7001
17/32"	.53125	13.493
9/16"	.5625	14.287
19/32"	.59375	15.081
5/8"	.625	15.875
11/16"	.6875	17.462
3/4"	.75	19.050
25/32"	.78125	19.843
7/8"	.875	22.2251
29/32"	.90625	23.0188
15/16"	.9375	23.8126
31/32"	.96875	24.6063
1"	1.0	25.4001

Glossary of Terms & Abbreviations

Aerometer	An instrument designed to measure air speed & volume.
AFCI	Arc Fault Circuit Interrupter
ANSI	The American National Standards Institute is a private nonprofit organization that oversees the development of voluntary consensus standards for products, services, processes, systems, and personnel in the United States.
ANSI Z87	Impact protector requirements for safety glasses.
ASME	The American Society of Mechanical Engineers is an American professional association
BAS/BMS	Building Automation System/Building Management System: HVAC, lighting, security automated controls.
BBP	Best Business Practice
BIM	Building Information Modeling is an intelligent 3D representation of the physical spaces and assets within a facility.
Blackwater	Water from toilets, urinals, and dishwashers. (Sewage)
BMMS	Building Maintenance Management System
Breakdown Maintenance	Wait for the equipment to fail, then fix it. (If it isn't broken, don't fix it.)
CAD	Computer Aided Drafting
Chalk Circle Observation	Taiichi Ohno is widely credited for the 'Chalk Circle' a technique of coaching the observation of a processes to identify waste (time, energy, procedure, etc.)
CMMS	Computerized Maintenance Management System tracks & schedules work orders.
Condition Monitoring	(CM) is the process of monitoring a particular condition in a piece of equipment such as vibration, temperature, etc. to identify changes that could indicate a developing fault. Data collection, data analysis, alert generation.
Contamination Control	A term for activities aiming to control the existence and proliferation of contamination in certain areas of a facility.
Corrective Maintenance	Correcting a problem with a piece of equipment in the moment. Unplanned.
EPA	Environmental Protection Agency
EPA Section 608	EPA regulations (40 CFR Part 82, Subpart F) Section 608 of the Clean Air Act require technicians who maintain, service, repair, or dispose of equipment that could release refrigerants into the atmosphere must be certified.
FM	Facilities Management
GFCI	Ground Fault Circuit Interrupter
Graywater a.k.a. Greywater	Water from sinks, bathtubs, showers, laundry.
HAZMAT	Hazardous Materials
HAZWASTE	Hazardous Waste
HAZWOPPER	Hazardous waste and emergency response plan/guidelines. General industry, 29 CFR 1910.120; and construction 29 CFR 1926.65)
KPI's	Key Performance Indicators
Latent Heat Capacity of an AC	Refers to how much moisture or water vapor it can turn into liquid water at the evaporator.
Lockout/Tagout (LOTO)	OSHA standard 29 CFR 1910.147 is designed to prevent injuries caused by the unexpected release of energy during maintenance.
Manometer	An instrument used to measure gas pressure.
Manual D	Used to size HVAC supply and return ducts
Manual J	Used for residential load calculation for sizing HVAC systems.
Manual S	A comprehensive guide for selecting and sizing residential heating, cooling, dehumidification, and humidification equipment
Mean time to repair (MTTR)	Mean Time to Repair (MTTR) refers to the amount of time required to repair a system and restore it to full functionality. MTTR = Total Maintenance Time / Number of Repairs.
MSDS	Material Safety Data Sheet
OSHA	Occupational Safety & Health Administration
Planned Maintenance	Maintenance activities that are planned, documented, and scheduled.
PO	Purchase Order
PPE	Personal Protective Equipment
Predetermined Maintenance	Follows a factory maintenance schedule.

Glossary of Terms & Abbreviations Cont.

Predictive Maintenance (PdM)	Utilizes condition-monitoring tools & techniques to track the performance of a piece of equipment. Data driven by preset parameters.
Preventative Maintenance (PM)	Regular maintenance tasks are performed on a working piece of equipment using tools/materials to reduce the chance of equipment failure. (Time-based & usage-based schedules.)
Psychrometer	A device for measuring air humidity (wet bulb).
Reactive Maintenance	Wait for the equipment to fail, then fix it. (If it isn't broken, don't fix it.)
Reclaiming Refrigerant	Sending recovered refrigerant to a facility to be purified back to virgin standards.
Recovering Refrigerant	Recovering Refrigerant into a tank.
Recycling Refrigerant	Running the refrigerant through filter dryers to clean and reuse it.
Reliability Centered Maintenance (RCM)	To identify the most effective maintenance techniques to control and prevent the risk of equipment failure & performance slowdowns.
RFI	Request for Information
RFP	Request for Proposal
RFQ	Request for Quote
ROI	Return on Investment
Routine Maintenance	Non-specialized maintenance tasks done on a regular basis, such as daily inspections to identify potential problems.
Run to Fail Maintenance (RTF)	Run a piece of equipment until it fails and requires repair or replacement.
Scheduled Maintenance	Maintenance activities that are planned, documented, and scheduled.
Sensible Heat Formula in HVAC	Airflow rate (in cfm) x (temperature differential between outgoing and entering air) x 1.08 equals sensible heating (in Btu/hr).
SDS	Safety Data Sheet
Sick Building Syndrome (SBS)	The sick building syndrome (SBS) is used to describe a situation in which the residents of a building experience health issues or discomfort after time spent in the building.
SOP	Standard Operating Procedures
Static Pressure in HVAC Ducts	The resistance to airflow within the air ducts.
Subcooling	The difference between the refrigerant's condensing temperature and the temperature of the liquid line is how much the refrigerant has cooled down after it has condensed into a liquid in the condenser. Liquid saturation temperature - Liquid line temperature = Subcooling
Superheat	The amount refrigerant vapor exceeds its boiling point. It's the extra heat added to the vapor so that it remains a gas state as it exits the evaporator coil. Suction line temperature - Suction saturation temperature = Superheat
SWPPP	Storm Water Pollution Prevention Plan
VPN	Virtual Private Network, increases data security by creating an encrypted connection between a device and the internet.
"W.C.	Inches of Water Column
WIP	Work in Process
Work Order (WO)	A formal document that provides detailed instructions and information about a specific maintenance or repair task.
5 W's	Who, What, Where, When Why. Strategic facility project planning tool.

AUTHOR BIO

Kevin Jones is a facilities professional with over twenty years of experience in the facilities maintenance space. Kevin took drafting all four years of high school, earning an R.O.P. certificate in AutoCAD. Kevin started his career in facilities maintenance in 2002 working for a heavy equipment company in SanDiego, CA. Kevin become a state certified general electrician, utilized his drafting skills to design custom shop equipment, learned to MIG weld so he could then fabricate custom shop equipment for his employer. Kevin also performed plumbing, electrical, and equipment repairs and maintenance for his employer. Kevin was instrumental in earning his company multiple waste reduction and recycling awards from the city of San Diego, as well as a W.R.A.P. award from the state of California for implementing: a mop water reclamation system, closed-loop wash rack water recycling system, an absorbent pad wringer, aerosol can recycling system, and an oil filter crusher.

After nearly thirteen years in San Diego, Kevin moved with his family to North Carolina where he found work as facilities maintenance technician. Kevin performed plant maintenance and operated the onsite greywater treatment plant. Kevin also worked as a metal fabricator, learning to stick weld and TIG weld. Kevin designed a socket weld valve leak testing device that was used to detect defective socket weld valves from the manufacturer, eliminating rework from defectively manufactured valves.

In 2019 Kevin and his family moved to Colorado, where he gained his state apprentice plumbing and electrician licenses. Kevin also earned his EPA Section 608 Universal HVAC Certification, and a Mech IV Heater Mechanic's License. As of 2024 Kevin was working as a building engineer for two commercial office buildings were he oversaw the installation of a new building automation system (BAS) and 160-ton chiller.

Kevin has a YouTube channel devoted to facilities maintenance here:
http://www.youtube.com/@kjfacilities-maint

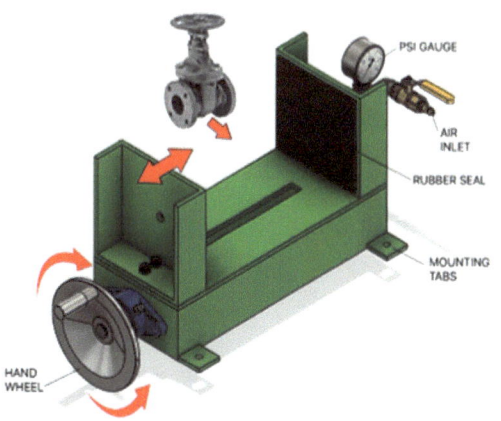

www.ingramcontent.com/pod-product-compliance
Lightning Source LLC
Chambersburg PA
CBHW061156030426
42337CB00002B/22